THE EXPERIENCE

Exhibition Guide

THE EXPERIENCE

Exhibition Guide

The 400th Anniversary of the King James Bible

Scott Th. Carroll

Director of the Green Collection

*Research Professor of Manuscript Studies and the Biblical Tradition,
Baylor University*

*Research Scholar, Robert C. Cooley Center for the Study of Early Christianity
Gordon-Conwell Theological Seminary, Charlotte.*

TRIANGLE PUBLISHING
Indiana Wesleyan University
Marion, Indiana

Passages: The Experience
Scott Th. Carroll, PhD

Direct correspondence and permission requests to one of the following:

E-mail: info@trianglepublishing.com

Web site: www.trianglepublishing.com

Mail: Triangle Publishing
Indiana Wesleyan University
1900 W. 50th Street
Marion, Indiana 46953
USA

Carroll, Scott
Passages: The Experience

ISBN-13: 978-1-931283-44-1
ISBN-10: 1-931283-44-3

Printed in the United States of America.

Passages

TABLE OF CONTENTS

If your glass is half empty, you probably have an app by which you track, with grim satisfaction, the ever-growing number of Christian denominations worldwide. The total is now approaching 40,000, no two of which read the Bible in the same way. Seen from this perspective, Scripture is above all something to argue about.

If, on the other hand, your glass is always at least half full, a different picture comes to mind: a third-century Syrian Christian, perhaps, sharing a pew with a recently converted Norseman, a student in Calvin's Geneva, a nun in the heyday of the Spanish Empire, a young widow in Uganda, and the pastor of a house church in China, brought together for worship that defies the boundaries of time and space, each of them reading or hearing the Bible in his or her own language.

In that spirit, and with its own striking cast of characters, *Passages* gives us vivid glimpses of the Bible's history, from its beginning in the Hebrew Scriptures to the present day. Central to this exhibition is a technology so familiar to us that we take it for granted: the book. And yet the book was once as radical, as disruptive, as the digital technology of the 21st century.

The "first commercial production of the Bible," the Exhibition Guide tells us, took place in Paris around 1230, "with the mass production of the Latin Vulgate Bible for university use." The exhibition features a Parisian Bible "probably intended for a traveling preacher." Although the Reformation was still almost three centuries away, the seeds for that revolutionary movement—emphasizing the need for individual believers to gain an intimate knowledge of Scripture—were already being sown. And in another three centuries—taking us to 1830—that "traveling preacher" might have been an itinerant Methodist in the backwoods of America. Where will his counterpart be preaching in 2130?

The most famous translation of the Bible, the King James Version, celebrated its 400th anniversary in 2011, an occasion marked by conferences throughout the United States and around the world. The exhibition takes us to the Jerusalem Chamber in Westminster Abbey, where the New Testament committee of the KJV translators "met for their final revision." If we listen carefully, the Exhibition Guide suggests, we might hear the ghosts of the translators, debating how best to convey the nuances of the original. At the same time, the exhibition honors modern-day translators for Wycliffe and similar organizations, men and women whose names will not be known, whose final revisions took place in utilitarian dwellings far removed from Westminster Abbey, who labored to render the Bible into languages that hadn't even been converted to writing before the translators began their patient study.

For various reasons, ranging from nuclear proliferation to forecasts of ecological catastrophe to certain ways of interpreting the Bible, many people are convinced that the end of history is near. Maybe they are right. But maybe not, and maybe a long future lies ahead as difficult for us to foresee as it would have been for Saint Jerome to imagine iPhones and Kindles. *Passages* doesn't provide a script for the future, but it does suggest how our descendants might get there: by twists and turns; by blood, sweat, and tears. The Bible appears here in many forms: annotated, explicated, translated, ornamented, illuminated, illustrated. But in all those forms it tells the same story, the Greatest Story Ever told—a story of creation and fall and redemption, a story that orients us, no matter where we're born or what the century may be, a story that tells us how to live.

John Wilson
Founding Editor, *Books & Culture*, a bimonthly review

Passages™

The creation of *Passages* has been the collaborative work of gifted and dedicated individuals. I want to begin by expressing my deepest appreciation to the Green Family for their trust, vision, support, and partnership in this venture. Nearly three hundred items from their extraordinary collection comprise the permanent exhibition and many more are on display in rotating exhibitions. Beyond the stunning collection, without their financial and personal support, *Passages* would not exist. Everyone involved in this project collectively expresses their thanks and appreciation to the Greens whom I know would respond with genuine and understated humility, saying, *"Soli Deo Gloria."*

Passages was created—from the concept to the opening—at warp speed: in just over seven months. Numerous people worked tirelessly on countless details. I want to recognize the indefatigable efforts of my coworkers. I appreciate beyond words the careful attention to countless details and the flawless work of Lauren McAfee, office manager; Amy Southerland, administrative assistant; Clifford Keister, facility manager; Allyson Bold and Cassie Summers, data entry specialists; Melody Winters, registrar; Joy Carroll, curator; and other staff members. The work would have been insurmountable without the support of numerous professionals at Hobby Lobby from many departments and especially Marsha Bold. I also want to express my appreciation for the work of the DeMoss Group for their public relations support and collaboration and the help of Jerry Pattengale, PhD, director of the Green Scholars Initiative. To all: my deepest appreciation and gratitude.

I also would like to express my appreciation to our various Boards for helping provide vision and direction and to Baylor University and to Gordon-Conwell Theological Seminary-Charlotte for collegial support, to academic colleagues, and to various collectors, all of whom have helped shape and bring definition to the collection and its use.

This exhibit would not exist without the work of Cary Summers and the creative and industrious people working with him through the Nehemiah Group. They implemented the historical settings and experiential aspects that make *Passages* come alive.

Above all, I want to thank my wife, Denise. Not only does she possess proofreading and editing skills, but her unfailing patience, support, and help has been invaluable to me. She also made the inestimable sacrifice of a fifteen-month separation that enabled me to launch this venture. Apart from visits few and far between, she believed in me and shared my dream that this might become a reality.

With humble appreciation and great joy,

Scott Th. Carroll, PhD

Remembering *Passages*

Thank you for coming to *Passages*, a celebration of the 400th anniversary of the publication of the King James Bible. As the name suggests, *Passages* is not your normal exhibition. It is a travel-through-time offering a behind-the-scenes glimpse as to how the most frequently copied, printed, quoted, sold, and banned book ever was preserved and adorned over time. After all, the Bible didn't just fall from heaven into Moses' lap on Mt. Sinai and mysteriously end up in the bedside drawer at the local hotel.

Prior to entering the exhibition, you may have taken time to listen to random interviews conducted on the street asking rather basic questions about the Bible. One might think that if the Bible is the best-selling book of all times, people ought to know a lot about it. The questions included: What is the first book of the Bible? What is the last book of the Bible? What is your favorite verse in the Bible? The interviews were not intended to ridicule or be demeaning to anyone. But some very interesting things came to light. First, that while the Bible is popular, there is a considerable lack of understanding about it. Second, despite the lack of knowledge, the vast majority of people interviewed believed it to be relevant for today. And finally, children often had a clearer understanding of the Bible than adults!

We hope that *Passages* will provide a clear understanding of the transmission of the Book of Books through time and an appreciation for the composition, preservation, and adornment of all books, and especially of the Bible, over time. We also want to underscore the incredible dedication—of time, work, economic investment, skills, education, and even loss of life—that people gave for something we often take for granted. Above all, we hope that this Guide to *Passages* might make your experiences at the exhibition and with the Bible more meaningful and memorable.

A note about the text: although it is traditional to refer to historical dates as BC and AD, we have chosen to use the less-customary BCE (Before Common Era) and CE (Common Era).

CHAPTER ONE

THE ANCIENT SYNAGOGUE

The Ancient Synagogue Exhibit Gallery

TIMELINE: The items in the synagogue date from around 900 BCE, or the time of King David, to the turn of the 20th century CE, illustrating nearly three millennia of Jewish tradition and religious and cultural continuity.

GEOGRAPHICAL RANGE: The items in this room originated in Israel and the Middle East, Europe, Asia, and Africa.

THE SETTING: The Dura-Europos Synagogue was uncovered at Dura-Europos, Syria, in 1932. An Aramaic inscription dates the last construction phase to 244 CE, making it one of the oldest synagogues in the world. Unlike other synagogues, it was preserved virtually intact. Of special importance are the wall paintings. The synagogue contained a forecourt and house of assembly with painted walls with biblical scenes, and a Torah shrine in the western wall facing Jerusalem. A scavenger hunt is available to try to identify scenes that adorned the walls of the synagogue.

Before the final Persian attack of the city in 256 CE, parts of the synagogue that abutted the western wall were filled with sand as a defensive measure, ironically preserving the synagogue and wall paintings. The reconstruction provides a stunning setting for the display of ancient Jewish writings which, like the synagogue, survived the ravages of time.

Our ornate Torah shrine contains a video screen that scrolls many of the 4,000 rules that a Jewish *sofer* (scribe)-in-training is required to memorize before being entrusted with the incalculable responsibility of copying God's very words. This was not the work of a novice or someone with little care for details. The rules were designed to reduce inadvertent errors. This room displays Jewish scrolls that span nearly two millennia and show the great care taken by the *sofer* and later correctors to ensure that the text was properly copied and transmitted to Jews and Christians alike.

Video docents introduce visitors to the *Passages* experience.

O Great God of Heaven
help the sofer *copy the text accurately*
and help the corrector be more accurate.
But, according to your great mercies to us,
help the corrector of the corrector be most accurate of all!
- A prayer found in the margin of a tenth-century Tanakh
(Hebrew Bible codex or book)

Genesis 32:3–7c Dead Sea Scroll Fragment, first century BCE

This fragment of the Dead Sea Scrolls contains one of the earliest-known texts of the Book of Genesis. The dating is based on handwriting analysis (paleography) and radiocarbon dating. The fragment contains seven clear lines of text written in a small Hebrew script. More than 27 fragments from the Book of Genesis have survived among the Dead Sea Scrolls, making it one of the more commonly attested books of the Hebrew Scriptures from the scrolls.

Prior to the discovery of the Dead Sea Scrolls between 1947 and the early 1960s, the Hebrew Old Testament text was based on medieval copies dating more than 1,200 years later than the earliest Dead Sea Scroll texts. Although study of the Dead Sea Scrolls indicates that different translations were in circulation at that time, it also shows that the text was transmitted over the ages with the greatest care.

1 Samuel 1, Greek LXX, early third century CE

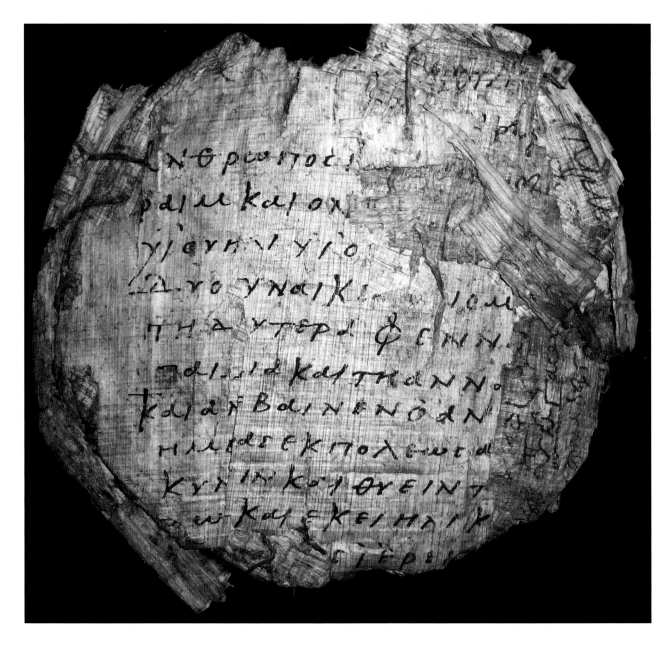

The Greek text of 1 Samuel is very important for two reasons. First, there is little surviving evidence for the Books of Samuel in Greek; this papyrus, discovered in Egypt, is part of a much larger fragmented manuscript that dates to the third century CE, more than 100 years earlier than the only other known papyrus text of that book. Second, the Greek text of Samuel is a translation of a lost Hebrew version that more closely aligns with the Dead Sea Scrolls than any other Greek translation of an Old Testament book.

This text and others from eight additional chapters of 1 Samuel were found in papyrus that had been pressed and sewn together and recycled for domestic use. Ironically, the biblical papyri were found with extensive texts of the most important religious writing of the ancient Greeks: Homer's *Iliad*. The people living in Middle Egypt frequently reused discarded papyri texts. The Greek translation of the Hebrew Scriptures, called the Septuagint (abbreviated LXX), was commonly used by Jews and Christians. Because this text is part of a book (codex), it was most likely used by Christians who readily adapted the text format, and it was used much later by Jews for their Scriptures.

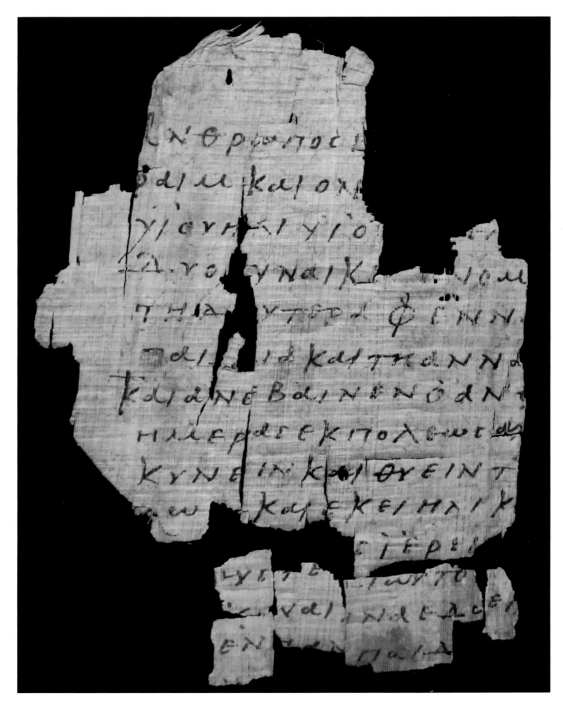

Papyrus text containing portions of 1 Samuel 1.

Spanish Inquisition Torah Scroll

This is a Sephardic Torah Scroll, meaning it is associated with the Jews predominately from the Iberian Peninsula (Spain and Portugal) and North Africa. *Torah* is a word meaning "law" and refers to the first five books of the Bible, the Pentateuch or Books of Moses, a core element of Jewish devotion and practice.

It is written on *gvil*, or a brown skin, which reflects a unique process for producing the parchment customary in these regions. Based on the style of writing, the scroll was very likely produced in northern Spain in the 14th century during the Spanish Inquisition, a period of harsh persecution of the Jews. Jews and Arabs were eventually expelled from Spain on the very day and from the very port that Columbus set sail on his maiden voyage of discovery.

The scroll has been dated based on the unique formation of letters distinct to the writing style used only at that time in that region. The great care taken by the *sofer* and correctors can be seen with all of the erasures made to correct the text.

Ashkenazi Esther Scroll, 16th century

This beautiful Esther Scroll, written on cream-colored, supple calfskin parchment, is missing the first skin. The Esther Scroll, along with several other short books, is often referred to as a Megillah (a roll). The ink is brown. The scroll was very likely produced in Germany and, based on the unique writing style, dates to the 16th century.

Small cantillation marks above the text function like musical notes for the singing of the scroll during the second reading on the morning of the Feast of Purim. This scroll, which celebrates the deliverance of the Jewish people from extermination, doubtless endured the horrors of the Nazi Holocaust and would have provided an especially relevant message of hope.

A unique menorah tik (case) with bronze images of the menorah candelabra—provenance uncertain, 18th century.

Extraordinary and extremely rare French tik—perhaps one of six known in the world, 19th century.

A festive hand-made Moroccan mantle (a fabric covering for the Torah) with a dedication shield and an embroidered rope and ball, 19th century.

This Torah shrine mosaic is from a synagogue at Tiberias. The Torah shrine is where the scroll is stored in the synagogue. The great Jewish Biblical scholar, Ben-Ashur lived in Tiberias.

BIOGRAPHY: Aaron ben-Moses ben-Asher was an influential Jewish *sofer* who died around 960 CE. He lived in the biblical city of Tiberias on the western shore of the Sea of Galilee. He came from a long line of illustrious Masoretic scribes. Ben-Asher had a tremendous influence on Hebrew grammar and scholarship. He has been credited with producing the most accurate version of the Masoretic (medieval Hebrew biblical) text, influencing all later copies of the Tanakh or Hebrew Bible.

CHAPTER TWO

THE MONASTIC SCRIPTORIUM

The Monastic Scriptorium Exhibit Gallery

TIMELINE: The items in the Cloister date from mummy portraits from the first century BCE to scriptural texts dating to within generations of Jesus and the apostles through to the 15th century, illustrating the great care that Christian scribes took in the transmission and study of the Bible.

GEOGRAPHICAL RANGE: The items in the Cloister originated in Egypt and the Sinai, present-day Turkey, Greece, and Western Europe including Italy, France, Austria, Germany, the Netherlands, and England.

THE SETTING: The Cloister is an inner colonnaded courtyard of a monastery that itself is sometimes called a cloister. The courtyard commonly surrounded a garden that was not covered by a roof. Monks or sisters would walk under the columned porch, protected from the environment and the outside world, praying, meditating on Scripture, and interacting with one another. Adjacent to the cloister on the inside of the monastery were rooms used for various activities. One of the rooms, called a scriptorium, from the Latin root "to write," was a place where books and, most important, Scripture was copied. The Evangelists, a term used for the authors of the Gospels, are frequently depicted writing under a portico (pillars) connected with a canopy to represent the connection between the authors, the copyists, and the monastery.

The work of the scriptorium was intimately associated with monastic education and discipleship. Monks and sisters were assigned books by their abbot or abbess to copy. They often kept notebooks containing their reflections on the assigned texts. This, in part, is how education worked until Gutenberg's revolution with the printing press, which created a radical disruption in this time-proven approach to education. The most commonly copied book was the Bible. Most books, religious or profane, that survived the medieval times in the Christian world survived because they had been copied in a scriptorium.

There were two approaches for copying texts. In some cases a reader would slowly read a text from a lectern while a number of scribes copied it, producing multiple copies at once. This is indicated by unique spelling mistakes that can only be explained by a person writing from dictation or by the accidental insertion of homonyms or even words that sounded alike. The more common method was for a single scribe to copy a text from a copy known as an exemplar. Pictures of the Evangelists show this process, often working from a scroll, symbolically representing an early text copying to a codex. The scribes followed rules and endeavored with the greatest care to copy the text before them. Innovation was not celebrated in this area or in medieval art. It was seen as an act of pride. Despite the survival of numerous biblical manuscripts, only in a few instances have the actual exemplars or texts that were copied survived. This gives a slight indication of how many more manuscripts of the Bible once existed.

Some may surmise that the hand copying of Scripture precariously introduced fluctuation in the text. Nothing could be further from reality, given the devotion of the scribes and the logistical complications of altering a hand-copied text that for practical purposes followed as closely as possible

the exemplar. Great care was taken, for example, to begin and end the text on the same line being copied. In addition, once copied, it would have been extremely difficult to insert or delete large portions of text. These skeptical ideas are based on modern assumptions of editing in a digital age. In actuality, apart from minor differences in word order, spelling, and updated vocabulary, the variations in the texts are readily quantifiable, the major ones representing 2 percent of the entire text and none having any bearing on essential teachings of Scripture.

Inside a small room in the scriptorium is a scribe's desk and table. A scrolling screen shows responsibilities of the monk—to be educated and to take the greatest care in the transmission of Scripture.

O reader, take note
While the hand that copied this text rots in the grave
the word copied lives forever!

- A common colophon (scribal note)
found in biblical manuscripts

A video docent monk pauses from his work to tell visitors about the toils of hand-copying texts.

Papyrus 39
(commonly designated as P39)

This magnificent half sheet, found in the Middle Egyptian city of Oxyrhynchus, is one of the earliest-known texts of the Gospel of St. John. It is the earliest papyrus that contains John 8:14–22 written in Greek dating to the mid-second to early-third centuries CE, based on handwriting analysis. The text is copied by a formal hand, doubtless a converted Greek scribe. It was once part of a magnificent codex containing only the Gospel of John. It is the earliest codex known with a surviving page number, seen in the upper left corner (page 71 in Greek) indicating that this was part of a very large and impressive papyrus codex (book) of the Gospel. The survival of seemingly less important details, such as the page number, helps scholars calculate with a great degree of accuracy what was contained previously, based on word counts per page.

The common, misconstrued notion that the earliest Christians were distracted by a wide variety of gospels that were supposedly rendered noncanonical or stripped of their presumed authority by the emperor and the church is not supported by this early evidence. Nor is the notion that the Gospel of John was compiled by a number of authors over a period of time. Within a century of the life of the author, St. John, entire copies of the Gospels were in circulation in the middle of Egypt, more than 1,000 miles from where the Gospel was composed. No similar evidence survives of this magnitude of the other so-called lost gospels. The text supports the earliest and best copies of the Gospel of John and shows the care of the scribe. It may be within a few copies of the very original by St. John.

Codex *Climaci Rescriptus*

These parchment leaves, 139 in total, comprise one of the earliest, extensive Bibles in the world. The black Syriac text consists of monastic works copied over recycled biblical books written in Palestinian Aramaic (commonly called CPA or Christian Palestinian Aramaic), the dialect most closely associated with Jesus' household language, and in Greek. In the photo of the manuscript leaf containing the underlying Greek text, the leaf has been turned 180 degrees so that the Greek text can be seen right-side up, making the Syriac text that was written over it appear upside down. The biblical texts were written in the late fourth through the sixth centuries CE, but the Aramaic was translated from an earlier Greek manuscript of Scripture, now lost. New developments in technology are bringing the underlying texts to life and providing a direct connection to the world of Jesus. The manuscript was discovered at the Monastery of Mt. St. Catherine's in the Sinai Peninsula.

Evanis Greek Pocket Gospels

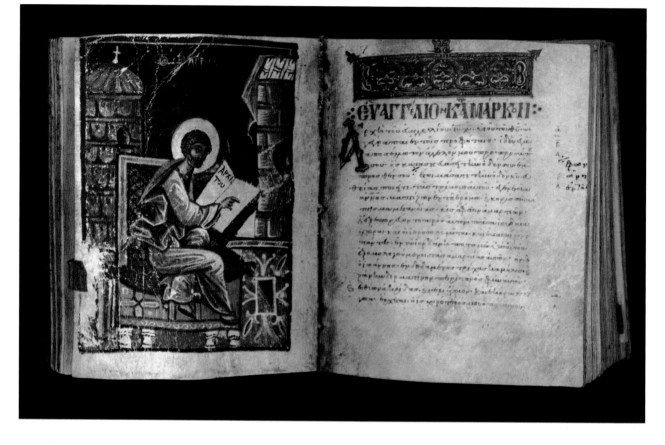

The codex containing the Gospels in Greek is one of the earliest examples of this style of writing, which would quickly become the primary script used by scribes. The script, called minuscule, provided a faster way of writing, including the abbreviation of letters rather than the previously used uncial script of capital letters. This so-called pocket Bible is one of the smallest Greek Gospels in the world, dating to around the tenth century. The portraits of the Evangelists, or the authors of the Gospels, were added later.

The ancient Gospels, like earlier texts of Scripture, do not indicate chapters or verses. The Gospels are divided into sections. Each section is preceded by cross-reference charts indicating to the reader where the same story in one Gospel can be found in another or whether the story is unique. Marginal references in the chart tell the reader if parallel passages can be found in other Gospels. The system was devised by the fourth-century church father Eusebius of Caesarea. Other marginal and textual annotations indicate the start and end of prescribed liturgical readings. Interestingly, this manuscript contains liturgical readings for Saturday and Sunday only, indicating that it must have been commissioned and cherished by a lay Christian who had secular responsibilities during the weekdays. This is a fascinating example of lay-readership of Scripture and devotion to it outside of professional churchlife.

Christianus' Commentary on the Gospel of St. Matthew

Christianus was an erudite Christian scholar of the ninth century. He lived and worked in the Carolingian Renaissance (beginning with Charlemagne) that celebrated, among other things, a careful reconstruction of Christian sources and celebrated biblical scholarship. Christianus was unique among scholars in the West who were working in Latin, because he had an intimate knowledge of Greek. Greek had been banned in the West when the Roman Church split from the Greek Church over theological and practical matters. In the commentary and in an effort to correct the Latin translation of Scripture, Christianus refers to Greek manuscripts available or known to him but now long lost.

This is the earliest-known complete text of this extremely

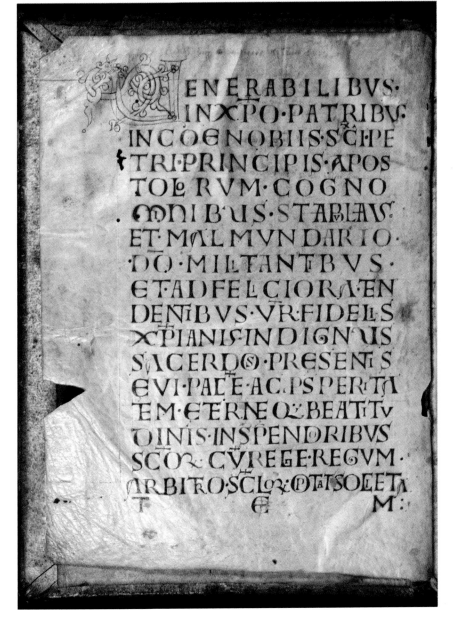

rare work. It was scripted in Bamberg, Germany, and dates to the early 11th century. It was likely copied from a manuscript dating close to the life of the Carolingian author. The presentation page is written in beautiful red Carolingian capitals and indicates that this was copied from an imperial manuscript, likely dating within centuries of the original composition. The love for the Bible and careful biblical scholarship were alive and well in the improperly dubbed Dark Ages.

Fayoum Portrait, first century BCE.

***Theon's Letter** containing specific references to Christianity at a time and place where it was vehemently persecuted, third century CE.*

A Christian scribe's inkwell and stylus, early fifth century CE.

Illumination in the Codex Amiantinus depicting Cassiodorus, the abbot, copying the Biblical text.

BIOGRAPHY: Flavius Magnus Aurelius Cassiodorus Senator (d. circa 585 CE), commonly known as Cassiodorus, was a Roman statesman and writer who lived in a tumultuous time after the fall of the Roman Empire in the West, serving in the administration of the king of the Ostrogoths. He came from southern Italy, where his father was the governor of Sicily. Cassiodorus was highly educated, had a reputation for keeping careful administrative records, and was entrusted with drafting important documents. In retirement he established a monastery at Vivarium on his family estate. Among his more notable writings are a work titled *Institutes*, which called for monastic training in Scripture and classical education, and a work encouraging the careful transmission of Scripture, titled *Of Scribes*. Copying Scripture became a holy obligation not relegated to those incapable of working elsewhere in the monastery but a privilege and responsibility of all. The copying of texts became the basis for monastic education.

CHAPTER THREE

ST. JEROME'S CAVE

St. Jerome's Cave Exhibit Gallery

TIMELINE: St. Jerome's Cave represents his time in Bethlehem learning Hebrew and Aramaic and translating the Scriptures into Latin from circa 382 to 405 CE. The items described in this setting are all Latin Bibles and commentaries dating from the middle of the ninth to the 15th centuries CE.

GEOGRAPHICAL RANGE: The items described in St. Jerome's Cave were composed in Italy, Germany, the Netherlands, France, and England.

THE SETTING: The area represents St. Jerome's Cave in Bethlehem. Jerome was commissioned by Pope Damasus I to create a new and reliable translation of the Bible into Latin for the common person. Though an accomplished scholar, he went to the Holy Land to learn Hebrew and Aramaic to more accurately translate the Scriptures into Latin. Previous Latin translations of Scripture were based on the Greek Septuagint (LXX). Jerome caught the vision to translate the Scriptures anew from the original languages. Many monks lived in caves in the hillsides surrounding Bethlehem. He thought there would be no better place to learn the language of the Lord than in the town of his birth. Jerome's trip and essential needs were underwritten by a wealthy supporter named Paula. The translation, called the Vulgate, was finished in the early fifth century and is considered the second-most-influential translation in history, second only to the King James Bible.

According to legend, all Jerome brought with him was his library, certainly of great value and no small effort to transport in the ancient world. He needed his "tools" to conduct the task he had been commissioned to do. Another legend claims that he occupied a cave that already had an imposing occupant: a Judean lion! According to the story, Jerome fearlessly removed a thorn from the lion's paw, thus forging a fast friendship. Jerome lived in the cave, and the lion guarded the library and translator; later artists depicted the lion as a sort of patron of Jerome.

Entering the cave, visitors encounter face to face the rather boisterous Louie the Lion. He is our personification of Jerome's legendary lion and the children's (and any willing adults') tour guide throughout the visit. Guests will also see Jerome, surrounded by his library, busy at work. Ask Jerome questions on a computer screen, and he will answer them, directly quoting from his copious writings. There is also a table with ink, quills, and texts to copy. Experience how difficult it is to copy a text by (electronic) candlelight as you help Jerome.

I not only admit but proclaim:
When translating the Greek, with exception to the Bible,
I don't translate word-for-word but sense-for-sense,
But my critics should also realize that while translating the Bible
One must consider the intent and not merely the literal words.

- St. Jerome's letter to Pammachius

St. Jerome sits in his cave working on his Vulgate translation of the Bible.

St. Cecilia Latin Bible

This is one of two surviving volumes from a Carolingian Bible scribed in Rome, dating to the ninth century. It is the earliest near-complete Latin Bible still owned privately. The magnificent manuscript is written in Latin on vellum in a Carolingian minuscule script. This volume contains Genesis 12:20 through Ruth with prologues and tracts by St. Jerome on Virginity. The text is written in two columns of 35 lines in a very fine hand by two scribes and includes seven large decorated initials in intertwined leaves and strap-work design.

The Carolingian Renaissance—a revival in the arts, architecture, intellectual pursuits, and religion—was led by a monk named Alcuin and his followers from Northumbria, England, who, in turn, were sponsored by Charlemagne, emperor of the Holy Roman Empire. There was also an attempt, attributed to Alcuin, to edit the Latin Vulgate and bring it into close alignment with the best surviving texts that dated back, close to the time of St. Jerome. He also reformed scribal practices, calling for greater care and attention to the transmission of the text.

Hattem Vulgate

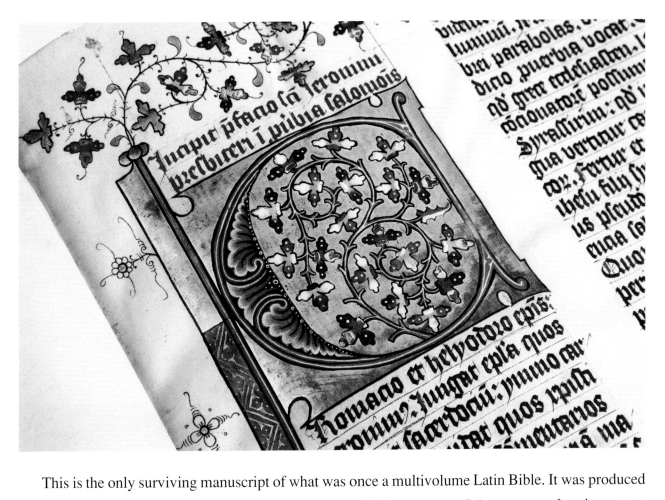

This is the only surviving manuscript of what was once a multivolume Latin Bible. It was produced in Hattem, the Netherlands, in the early 15th century. This was one of the centers of an important proto-reform movement called the *Devotio Moderna* or the Brothers and Sisters of the Common Life. The movement, with houses for men and for women, was founded by Geert Groote in the later 14th century. The movement called for reforms in the church, was dedicated to the education of children, emphasized a life of prayer and meditation, and was committed to the careful transmission of a Latin Bible that had been edited as closely as possible to the original translation by St. Jerome. Several efforts were made by members of the group to translate the Scriptures into the vernacular (regional non-Latin languages).

This particular biblical text is of enormous importance even though the remaining volumes have not survived. The manuscript provides early evidence for the movement's desire to restore a more reliable text of the Vulgate, and it survives from one of the centers for the movement. It is open to a beautiful, gilded illuminated capital.

Latin New Testament from England

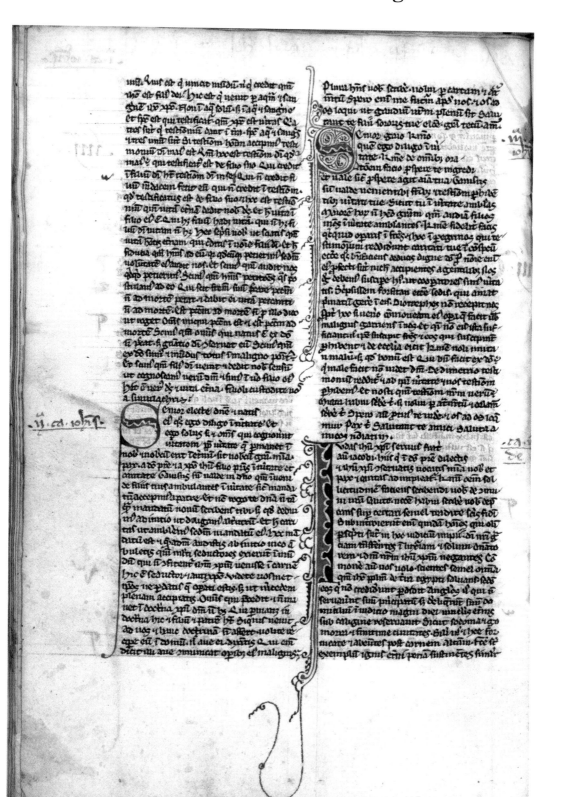

(Page Left) This is a complete, portable New Testament probably used by a traveling preacher. It is written on very thin and supple vellum made from "uterine calf skin"—from calves taken from the womb or stillborn; in either case, an extremely costly process. The manuscript was produced circa 1230–1260 in England. Each book is preceded by a prologue ascribed to St. Jerome that begins with a large red capital with decorative features. Capitals are decorated with flourishes. The text in this New Testament frequently follows readings from the Latin Bible that predates the early-fifth-century Vulgate translation by St. Jerome, indicating that the manuscript was copied from an exemplar that had preserved these earlier readings (called the *Vetus Latina* or Old Latin). The margins are filled with hundreds of editorial marks indicating textual anomalies or inconsistencies with the Vulgate text as it was traditionally scribed in the 13th century.

Proto-reform movements, like those led by John Wycliffe in England and Jan Hus in Bohemia, gravitated to these pre-Vulgate manuscripts. They presumed them to be untainted by the corruptions of the later medieval church and Vulgate Bible. This New Testament provides an interesting example of the sort of Latin text that would have been used by itinerant or traveling preachers and students around the time of Wycliffe.

Anselm of Laon's Commentary on Psalms, France, late 12th century.

Leber Atelier Parisian Bible, 1230

One of the most important developments in medieval book production occurred around 1230 in Paris, with the mass production of the Latin Vulgate Bible for university use. This was the first commercial production of the Bible. The format and the text were standardized in the process. A number of these features are still present in the modern versions of the Bible, demonstrating the far-reaching influence of these innovations. This particular Bible, however, reveals some anomalies. Biblical books appear in a different order and chapters were added later, indicating that this was an early example of the Parisian Bible. When Gutenberg chose to print a Bible that people were familiar with and would desire to purchase, he selected the Parisian Bible, introducing a new level of conformity.

The manuscript contains 79 historiated initials (decorated initials populated with a person or people), most opening a biblical book, on highly burnished grounds (an artistic phrase for a polished, shimmering gold background for the letter). Based on the style, it was likely illuminated by artists commissioned by the monarch, but the Bible was probably intended for a traveling preacher. It includes 80 themes for sermons written in red with scriptural quotations.

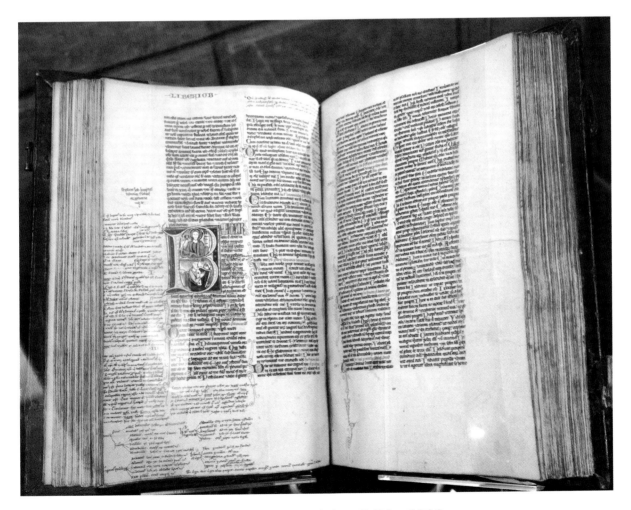

Leber Atelier Parisian Bible, 1230.

St. Jerome's Letters, Italy, early 15th century.

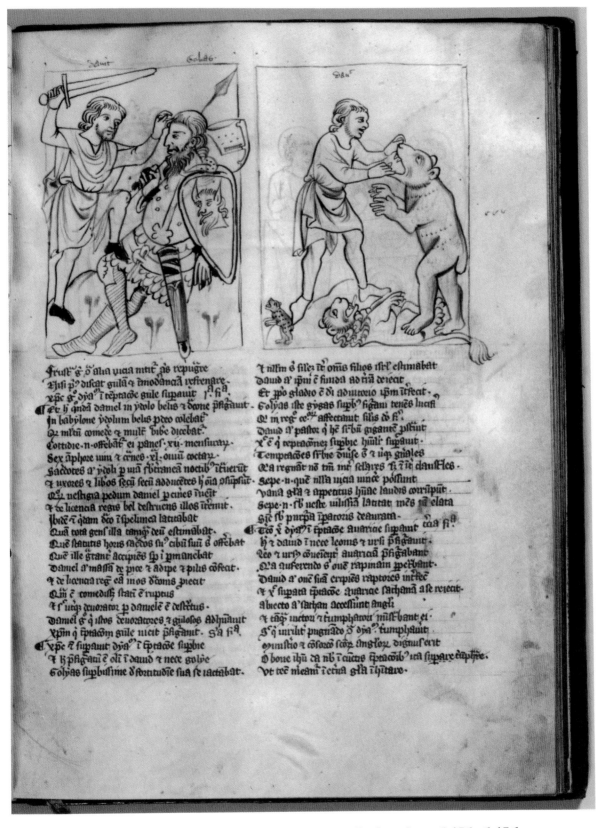

Nicolas de Lyra's Postilla, Ferarra, Italy, circa 1451–1456.

BIOGRAPHY: St. Jerome (d. 420) was from the border of ancient Dalmatia and Pannonia in the Balkans. He was a scholar, priest, monk, translator, and prodigious author of numerous works on polemics, theology, and historical topics, some in the form of letters and commentaries. He is best known for his translation of the Latin Bible, known as the Vulgate, from a word meaning "in the common language" or "intended for popular use."

In Jerome's day the version of the Latin Bible was called the *Vetus Latina* or Old Latin Bible, the Old Testament having been translated from the Greek Septuagint (LXX). Versions of the translations varied widely and often contained extra material. This

An engraving depicts St. Jerome in prayer, accompanied by his lion, surrounded by his work.

was extremely problematic given the theological controversies that were afoot at that time. Jerome was commissioned by Pope Damasus I (d. 384) to produce a new and reliable translation of the Latin Bible. The work that began in 382 was completed in 405 CE. Jerome moved to Bethlehem in 384 CE to learn Hebrew and Aramaic for the translation project. He was supported by a wealthy Roman benefactress named Paula. Jerome learned Hebrew and Aramaic from a Jewish convert. His translation of the Old Testament was derived from the Hebrew and Aramaic, raising criticism from those who thought the Greek Septuagint was inspired. Jerome produced two separate translations of Psalms, one translated into Latin from Hebrew and another translated from Greek because the Roman Church used this later version in its liturgy. Jerome's Vulgate has been used for a longer period of time than any other translation of Scripture.

CHAPTER FOUR

THE PEASANTS' VILLAGE

The Peasants' Village Exhibit Gallery

TIMELINE: The Peasants' Village represents the late medieval period in Europe dating from approximately 1300 to 1400. The items on display are more broadly represented in time beginning with a Coptic Papyrus of Psalms dating to the early fourth century CE and ranging to an Armenian Gospels dating to the 17th century.

GEOGRAPHICAL RANGE: The items in the Peasants' Village are arranged geographically by case. One case contains items from North Africa and Ethiopia. Another contains items from the Middle East, Eastern Europe, and Asia. Another contains items from Western Continental Europe, while the final case displays items from England.

THE SETTING: As guests enter the Peasants' Village, they pass between two small houses. Two hard-working women talk through the windows; they have a simple faith. The plague is raging, and there is a fear of death and eternity. Their discussion turns to religion.

One woman wonders how hope can be gained when people can't understand the Mass or Scripture in Latin.

Despite her expressions of frustration, she is faithful to the church and resigned to the way things are.

The other woman is bright-eyed, filled with hope and optimism despite being surrounded by death. She shares a secret with her neighbor about a translation of the Bible into English intended for regular people to understand the promises of God. She tells her friend that the translation was done by a churchman named John Wycliffe and his friends. She knows that the translation has been condemned, and people are taking a huge risk for the privilege of reading the Scriptures in their mother tongue. She invites her friend to a meeting where Wycliffe's Scriptures will be read.

But her friend will have nothing to do with it. She's a survivor, at least in this life, and won't put herself or her family at risk by being associated with a dangerous, condemned translation of the Bible. She can't understand Latin, but she does understand the threat of death at the stake. This brief dialogue establishes the time period for the Peasants' Village, the inability of most to understand Latin, and the desire (despite the threat of execution), to get the Scriptures in their everyday language. Louie the Lion hides in a well, ready to tell the children about the cool things in the Peasants' Village.

The friars and their followers say it's heresy
to have the Bible in English and to make it known to the unlearned.
Doesn't it seem right that the Bible should be taught in a language that's known?
Isn't that why St. Jerome toiled and translated the Bible from ancient languages into
Latin so that it might be translated into other modern languages?
It's really out of fear they don't want the Bible in English, because commoners would
understand the heresy being pawned-off on them.

- John Wycliffe, *On the Pastoral Office*

It is a dangerous thing, as blessed St. Jerome realized,
to translate the text of the Bible from one language to another
because the original sense is often lost.
So we issue this law: No one without proper permission
can translate any portion of the Bible into English or any other language
and that no one is permitted to read these unauthorized translations.

- Thomas Arundel, archbishop of Canterbury,
The Constitutions of Oxford, 1408

A traveling salesman, hawking
his wares, describes events
in Wycliffe's time.

The Roseberry Rolle, The Psalms and Canticles in Pre-Wycliffite English Translation, with Commentary by Richard Rolle, late 14th to early 15th centuries

This manuscript preserves one of the earliest, most extensive surviving texts of the Scripture in (Middle) English; the text, translation, and commentary of Richard Rolle (d. 1349) of the Psalms and Canticles with other original compositions preceded Wycliffe's famous translation of the Bible by nearly 40 years. This manuscript is also one of the most important surviving witnesses to the original autograph of the work by Rolle. It begins imperfectly at Psalm 17 and is missing a few pages in the middle. The tract ends with a Discussion of the Sacraments, a text on Theological Virtues, and the Fourteen Articles of Faith, as well as the Twelve Degrees of Meekness, all in (Middle) English, the latter in rhyming couplets.

Richard Rolle was an important English religious writer and Bible translator. He lived as a hermit in Yorkshire. Late in life he transferred his cell to Richmondshire, where he wrote a number of works in Latin and English and attended to the Cistercian nuns of Hampole until his death. Because they knew Latin only imperfectly and the Psalms were an integral part of their religious devotions, they appealed to Rolle for a translation they could understand. Rolle's text had a profound impact later on Wycliffe and his followers, and his renderings can even be found incorporated, doubtless subconsciously, in the King James Bible.

Illuminated Wycliffe New Testament, early 15th century

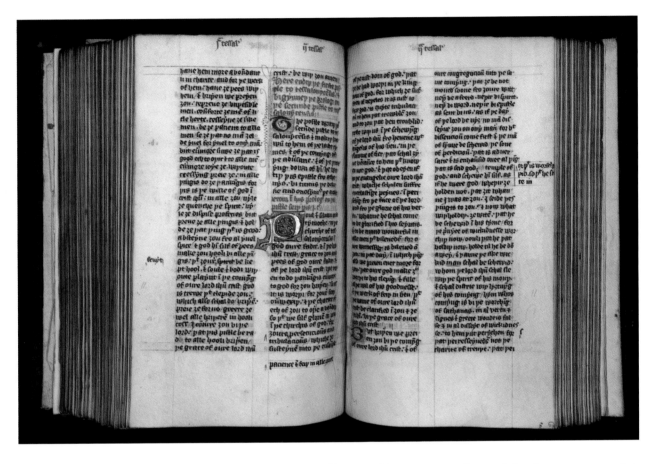

This is an unrecorded manuscript of the Wycliffe New Testament and certainly the most complete and among the most impressive in private hands in the world. Wycliffe's desire to produce the Bible in (Middle) English and its subsequent and aggressive repression ignited reform in England and was a major impetus for the later translation of the Bible into English.

John Wycliffe (d. 1384) and his colleagues undertook the first complete translation of the Bible into (Middle) English from the Latin Bible from the 1370s to around 1390. His followers were known as Lollards. Wycliffe's teachings were condemned in 1377 and in 1382. In the Constitutions of 1407 and in 1409, Thomas Arundel, archbishop of Canterbury, condemned unauthorized Bible translations and the ownership of translations was forbidden unless they predated Wycliffe or the owner had a license from the church for the translation. Possession of a Wycliffe Bible could be taken as evidence of heresy and might lead to prosecution, imprisonment, and being condemned to burn to death at the stake. The present manuscript was copied at a time when there were strict prohibitions against the Wycliffe Bible. It is distinguished by its large format and illuminated initials—a bold statement in times of trouble. Around 250 Wycliffite Bibles are known, with fewer than 15, including this one, in collections in the United States. More manuscripts survive of Wycliffe's Bible than any other (Middle) English work, including Chaucer's *Canterbury Tales*.

John Purvey, The True Copye of a Prolog Written about Two Hundred Yeres Paste, 1550

The true copye
of a Prolog wzytten about two C.
yeres paste by John Wycklife (as maye
iustly be gatherid vt that, that John Bale
hath wzitté of him in his boke entitlid the
Summarie of famouse wziters of the Ile
of great Britã) the Originall whereof
is founde wzitten in an olde Englifh
Bible bitwixt the olde Testament
and the Newe. Whych Bible
remaynith now in ý kyng
hys maiesties
Chamber.

✱✱✱

✱INNER✱TEMPLE✱

℄ Impzinted at London by Robert Crowley dwellynge in Elie
rents in Holburn. Anno Do.
MDL.

℄ Cum priuilegio ad impzi-
mendum solum.

This is an important and extremely interesting early edition of the Prologue to the Wycliffe Bible, written by one of the translators and later editors of the Wycliffe Bible, John Purvey (d. 1428). It was falsely attributed to Wycliffe (d. 1384). Purvey provides fascinating insight into the translation project, the translators' driving passion to make the Bible available in the vernacular, and the importance of Bible reading. Early Protestant translators found inspiration and a historical precedent in this popular work. Two earlier editions of this text taken from another manuscript were published in 1536 and 1540 under the title: Dore of Holy Scripture. A 1550 edition was derived from a different manuscript, allegedly from a Wycliffe Bible in the king's chamber.

Purvey summarizes the contents of the biblical books and provides information about the author and intersperses practical advice about biblical interpretation. He contends that it was God's will for the Scriptures to be read in the vernacular. He provides fascinating information about the translation of the Wycliffe Bible and the difficulties and challenges that the translators faced with this ominous and dangerous undertaking. He states that the translators edited a number of ancient copies of the Latin Bible and other works, which they recognized had been corrupted over time, to create their own reliable Latin text, from which they worked as they translated into (Middle) English. He also refers to their use of the popular commentary called the Postilla by Nicolas de Lyra as a way of trying to clarify the meaning of the Hebrew text of the Old Testament. Purvey explains that the translators decided to provide what is often called a dynamic-equivalent rendering or "sense for sense" rendering rather than a literal translation. Purvey ends with an ominous and prophetic prayer, "May God in his mercy help our people understand the Bible and obey it, whether in life or unto death!"

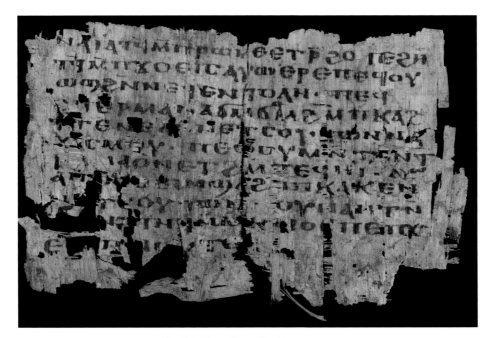

Sahidic Coptic Papyrus
Psalm 111:1-4 with a magical text, 320-350 CE.

Foxe's *Book of Martyrs,* 1563

This is the first edition of one of the most important and influential historical works of the English Reformation. The work is filled with primary sources and woodcuts graphically illustrating the martyrdoms vividly described in detail in the work. It replaced the medieval martyrdom accounts found in the Golden Legend with a new heavenly host of revered saints. It is also filled with now-lost primary sources providing gripping accounts of heroism and faith. The page shows Wycliffe's skeletal remains being exhumed, incinerated, and the ashes dispersed in a river as an attempt to deny a resurrection to life everlasting.

The work particularly emphasizes the sufferings of English Reformers from the 14th century through the persecution during the reign of Queen Mary Tudor I. The book was lavishly produced and illustrated with woodcuts and numerous decorated initials. It was by far the largest and most complicated publishing project in England to that time. The book captivated the hearts and imagination of Protestants and galvanized a spirit of resilience rooted in horrific and heroic accounts of martyrdom. Like many reform movements in church history, it sought to find authority by tracing a tradition and legitimacy through the blood of the martyrs.

French Psalms, 14th century.

Armenian Gospel Book, 12th–15th centuries.

BIOGRAPHY: John Wycliffe (d. 1384) was an English scholar, philosopher, minister, translator, and reformer. His protests against papal authority, transubstantiation, the suppression of the vernacular Scriptures in (Middle) English, and other abuses of the church anticipated some of the main issues of the Protestant Reformation by a century and a half. He has been called the Morning Star of the Reformation. His followers were called Lollards. Wycliffe's ideas were condemned by the church, and after his death his followers were condemned.

Wycliffe believed that the life of faith necessitated an intimate knowledge of the Bible that was not possible when the populace did not know Latin and Scripture was not readily available in Middle English. Wycliffe and a circle of friends translated the Latin Vulgate into Middle English in the early 1380s. One of Wycliffe's younger collaborators, John Purvey, revised the translation in the 1390s, making it more readable. The king of England and Archbishop of Canterbury William Arundel condemned the Lollards and Wycliffe's translation in various acts between 1401 and 1410. They even ordered Wycliffe's remains to be exhumed and incinerated, dispersing his ashes. Despite the attempted suppression, the Lollard movement continued to grow, as did the demand for the Bible in English. More copies of the Wycliffe Scriptures survive than any other work written in (Middle) English.

CHAPTER FIVE

GUTENBERG'S PRINT SHOP

Passages: THE EXPERIENCE

Gutenberg's Print Shop Exhibit Gallery

TIMELINE: Gutenberg's Print Shop was active throughout the last half of the 15th century, long after the original owner died. The items on display in the Print Shop range from a Buddhist prayer scroll printed in Japan in 770 CE to a so-called post-incunable printing of John Fisher's Fruitful Sayings of the Seven Psalms of David, 1525.

GEOGRAPHICAL RANGE: The items on display in Gutenberg's Print Shop were produced in Japan, North Africa, Germany, Italy, Spain, France, the Netherlands, and England.

THE SETTING: This is Gutenberg's Print Shop. In the corner of the room is an exact replica of Gutenberg's printing press, made of hand-crafted elm with a wooden screw. The press is fully functional. Gutenberg's apprentices are busy operating the press, printing replica pages of the Gutenberg Bible. It is a two-man job, but Gutenberg could have employed as many as 25 workers. It would likely take a compositor a day to set a page of type, backwards. One worker inks the composited pages while the other sets the paper and shuttles it under the press. The apprentice may call for help from a bystander in the shop to operate the press. It takes some muscle to pull the impressions. The press exerts more than 500 pounds of pressure per square inch. Watch out for the recoil!

The shuttle is pulled back, and the prints are carefully inspected. Good prints are hung between the twines of a rope to dry. The ink needs to be cleaned periodically from the composited pages. The process was more complicated when two or three colors of ink were used. A two-volume book such as the Gutenberg Bible consisted of hundreds of bifolia, or double pages, which needed to be printed on both sides. They did not follow in consecutive order, so the process was very complicated. Printers had multiple presses operating at the same time. While it was costly and painstaking, it accelerated the speed at which books could be produced. It also immediately standardized texts of Scripture.

The word *incunable* comes from a word that means "out of the cradle" and refers to the infancy era of printing. The incunable period is generally considered to span from around 1450 to 1500. This coincided with the Renaissance in Europe. Reading was democratized and learning vastly expanded. It was not by mistake that the Bible was the first book printed with movable typeset in the West. There is also a close relationship

An exact replica of a Gutenberg printing press with its wooden screw

between the expansion of learning, the publication of biblical and historical texts, and the call to reform abuses in the church.

Tables in the Print Shop are arranged for people to ink and print exact replica stamps of the block book on display. Block books were made from woodcuts that were used to create ready-made, simple books.

An apprentice in Gutenberg's print shop describes how the printing press works.

It's only a press, but a press from which
will flow a constant stream.
Through it, God will spread His Word.
A spring of truth will flow from it.
Like a new star it will scatter the darkness of ignorance
and cause an unknown light to shine for all.

- Johannes Gutenberg

The Antichrist and the 15 Signs of Doomsday, 1470

This is the only recorded, complete copy of this edition of this block book, which is an early form of printing that predates Gutenberg's use of movable typeset printing. The text was compiled from earlier writers by an anonymous editor. It contains 38 leaves and 54 illustrations. Block books allowed for new copies to be printed on request—comparable to the modern concept of "publishing on demand"—as opposed to the more tedious and time-consuming movable typeset printing.

The texts, which are incorporated in the block, were printed in German to make them accessible to laypeople. The book consists of a cycle of illustrations with explanatory texts. It tells the story of the antichrist who is described in the last book of the Bible, Revelation, as deceiving humans in the End Days by posing as Christ. His defeat is followed by the Last Judgment, depicted with illustrations containing alarming detail.

A Noble Fragment of the Gutenberg Bible, 1454

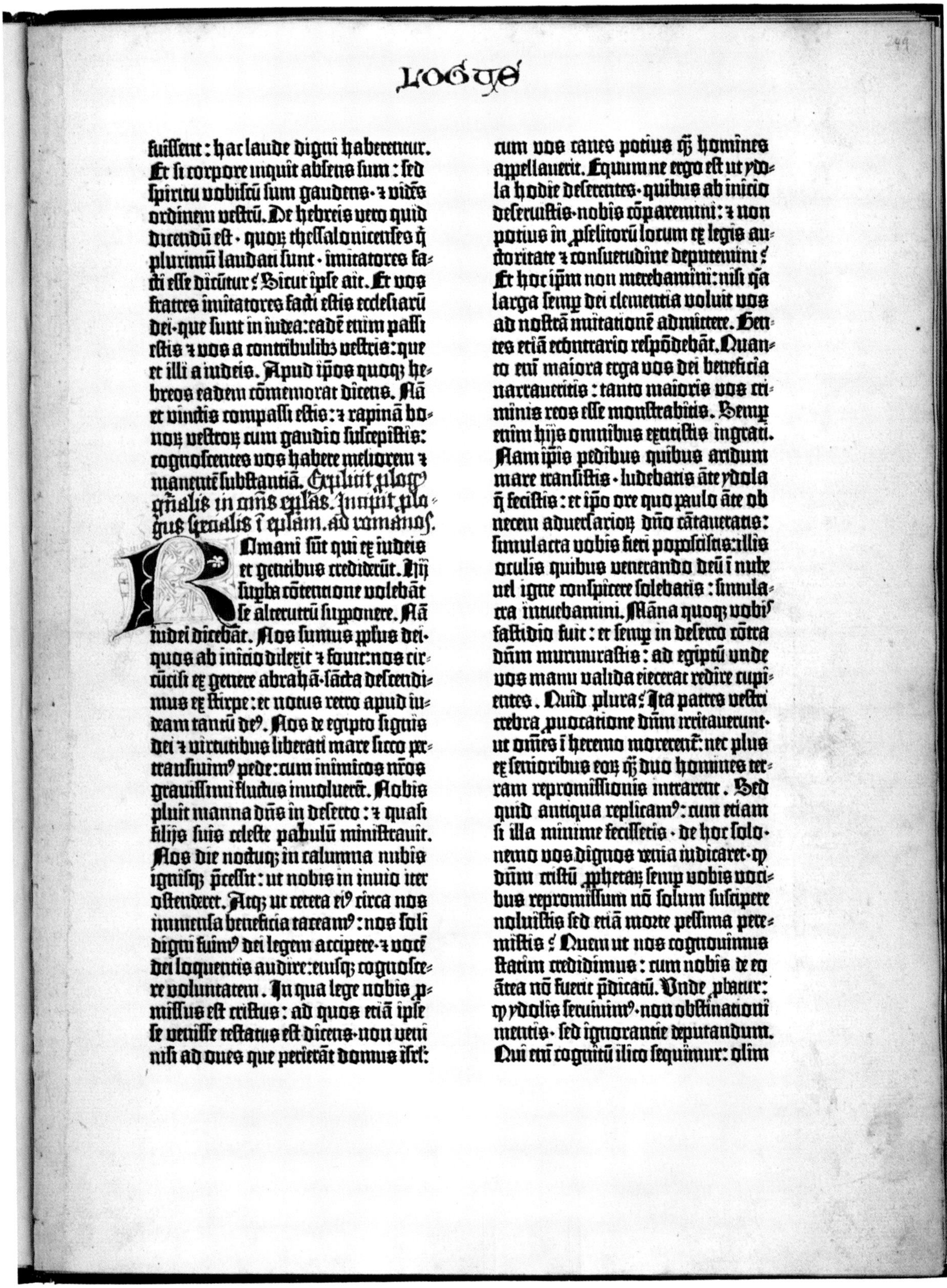

fuissent: hac laude digni haberentur.
Et si corpore inquit absens sum: sed
spiritu vobiscū sum gaudens · 𝜏 videns
ordinem vestrū. De hebreis vero quid
dicendū est · quoꝝ thessalonicenses q̄
plurimū laudati sunt · imitatores facti esse dicūtur? Sicut ipse ait. Et vos
fratres imitatores facti estis ecclesiarū
dei · que sunt in iudea: eadē enim passi
estis 𝜏 vos a contribulib; vestris: que
et illi a iudeis. Apud ipos quoq; he-
breos eadem cōmemorat dicens. Nā
et vinctis compassi estis: 𝜏 rapinā bo-
noꝝ vestroꝝ cum gaudio suscepistis:
cognoscentes vos habere meliorem 𝜏
manentē substantiā. Explicit plog'
gn̄alis in om̄s ep̄las. Incipit plo-
gus specialis ī ep̄lam ad romanos.
ROmani sūt qui ex iudeis
et gentibus crediderūt. Hij
superba cōtencione volebāt
se alterutrū supponere. Nā
iudei dicebāt. Nos sumus ꝑplus dei ·
quos ab inicio dilexit 𝜏 fouit: nos cir-
cūcisi ex genere abrahā · sācta descendi-
mus ex stirpe: et notus retro apud iu-
deam tantū deꝰ. Nos de egipto signis
dei 𝜏 virtutibus liberati mare sicco pe-
transiuimꝰ pede: cum inimicos nr̄os
grauissimi fluctus inuoluerit. Nobis
pluit manna dn̄s in deserto: 𝜏 quasi
filijs suis celeste pabulū ministrauit.
Nos die noctuq; in columna nubis
ignisq; p̄cessit: ut nobis in inuio iter
ostenderet. Atq; ut cetera eiꝰ circa nos
immensa beneficia taceamꝰ: nos soli
digni fuimꝰ dei legem accipere · 𝜏 vocē
dei loquentis audire: cuiusq; cognosce-
re voluntatem. In qua lege nobis ꝑ-
missus est cristus: ad quos etiā ipse
se venisse testatus est dicens · non veni
nisi ad oues que perierāt domus isrl̄:
cum vos canes potius q̄ homines
appellauerit. Equumne ergo est ut ydola hodie deserentes · quibus ab inicio
deseruistis · nobis cōparemini: 𝜏 non
potius in ꝓselitorū locum ex legis au-
ctoritate 𝜏 consuetudine deputemini?
Et hoc ipm̄ non merebamini: nisi q̄a
larga semꝑ dei clementia voluit vos
ad nostrā imitationē admittere. Gen-
tes etiā econtrario respōdebāt. Quan-
to eni maiora erga vos dei beneficia
narraueritis: tanto maioris vos cri-
minis reos esse monstrabitis. Semꝑ
enim hijs omnibus extitistis ingrati.
Nam ipis pedibus quibus aridum
mare transistis · ludebatis āte ydola
q̄ feceratis: et ipo ore quo paulo āte ob
necem aduersarioꝝ dn̄o cātaueratis:
simulacra vobis fieri poposcistis: illis
oculis quibus venerando deū i nube
vel igne conspicere solebatis: simulacra intuebamini. Māna quoq; vobis
fastidio fuit: et semꝑ in deserto cōtra
dn̄m murmurastis: ad egiptū unde
vos manu valida eiecerat redire cupi-
entes. Quid plura? Ita patres vestri
crebra ꝓuocatione dn̄m irritauerunt ·
ut om̄es ī heremo morerent̄: nec plus
ex senioribus eoꝝ q̄ duo homines ter-
ram repromissionis intrarent. Sed
quid antiqua replicamꝰ: cum etiam
si illa minime fecissetis · de hoc solo
nemo vos dignos venia iudicaret · q
dn̄m cristū ꝓphetaꝝ semꝑ vobis voci-
bus repromissum nō solum suscipere
noluistis sed etiā morte pessima pere-
mistis? Quem ut nos cognouimus
statim credidimus: cum nobis de eo
antea nō fuerit p̄dicatū. Unde ꝓbatur:
q ydolis seruiuimꝰ · non obstinationi
mentis · sed ignorantie deputandum.
Qui eni cognitū ilico sequimur: olim

A Noble Fragment of the Gutenberg Bible, 1454 (continued)

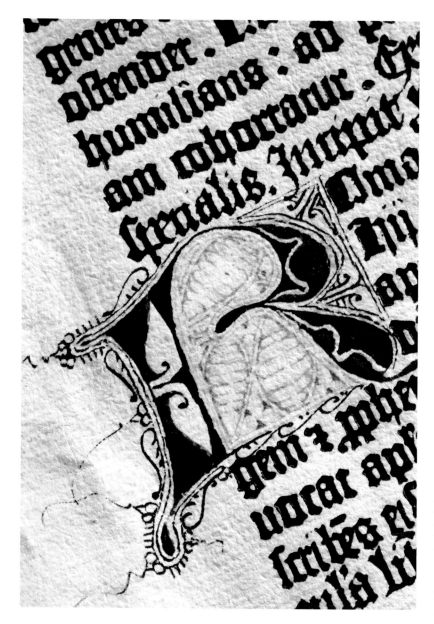

Johannes Gutenberg (d. 1468) created an innovative way to print with a press and movable typeset print that would become a standard approach to printing for more than 350 years. As a goldsmith, Gutenberg had the ability to create metal fonts for each letter of the alphabet and character used in writing. His font consisted of about 290 different characters, including 47 capital letters, 63 lowercase letters, and many combinations of letters used by medieval scribes, abbreviations, punctuation marks, and even spaces. The letters were set by hand for each page and then reused. The fonts were designed to lock together and then unlock and were hard enough to withstand thousands of impressions. The press was modeled after the wine presses in the surrounding region of Mainz.

Gutenberg borrowed money from the financier Johann Füst who, with a second loan to Gutenberg, invoked a partnership "in the production of books." Gutenberg was unable to repay his debts before he could sell the Bibles. Füst foreclosed on the loans and took possession of everything Gutenberg had created. Füst then went into partnership with Gutenberg's most capable employee, Peter Schöffer, who later married Füst's daughter. The two became the most renowned printers of their day. According to some stories, Gutenberg died penniless in debtors' prison, forgotten, yet his innovation has been commemorated as one of the most significant and influential developments in history. Approximately 35 copies of Gutenberg's Bible were printed by him on vellum and 150 copies on paper. Forty-eight copies have survived in various states of repair; only 20 of the copies are complete. In addition, approximately 65 single leaves and fragments are kept in 30 collections worldwide.

Füst-Schöffer Fourth Latin Bible, 1462

This is an extremely rare fourth edition of the Latin Bible printed by Gutenberg's leading apprentice, Peter Schöffer, and his financier, Johann Füst, who foreclosed on Gutenberg and took over his shop. The edition was printed in two volumes on Gutenberg's press with a more readable font created by Schöffer. Only four copies survive in this condition: printed on vellum, illuminated, and in their original bindings.

The picture shows the end of the prologue and opening of Genesis. A magnificent magenta band filled with delicate white designs and banded with gold decorates the inner margin of the page with vines, leaves, and blossoms in red, blue, green, and purple with highlights of gold. The impression is that the vine is growing

around the page. God is at the top overseeing creation. A monkey sits on a vine and a beautiful bird perches on the tendrils. Latin medieval Bibles often had a standardized creation scene that accompanied the opening of Genesis. This is a fascinating rendition of creation with God at the top overlooking, as if supervising, the orb that represents the universe while the vegetation grows around the margins filled with animals.

Wynken de Worde's *Golden Legend*, 1493

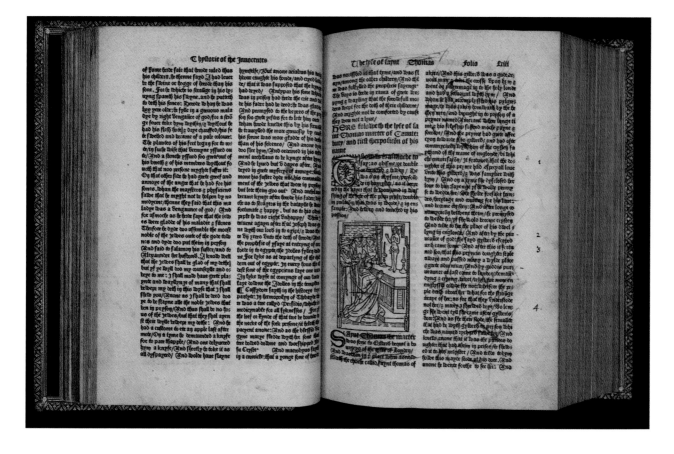

 The Golden Legend is a collection of "lives of the saints," arranged according to the liturgical calendar. The original work, usually referred to as the *Legenda Aurea*, was compiled in Latin between 1250 and 1280 by Jacobus de Voragine, archbishop of Genoa. While originally intended to be a manual for preachers, it swiftly became a popular book for private devotion and inspiration. Over 1,000 manuscripts are extant. The decision to publish (print) it was a brilliant choice. The Latin text enjoyed a distribution success second only to the Bible through the 16th century.

 The work was originally published in English by Caxton in 1483 and later by Wynken de Worde and Julian Notary, both former apprentices of Caxton's. Each incorporated biblical texts in English in the legends—illegally and at great risk. These bold attempts to distribute Scripture in English surreptitiously are often overlooked. The work is lavishly illustrated with woodcuts executed by two artists. Overtly Catholic portions of this copy have been defaced by a Protestant owner. The picture shows Christ surrounded by a cloud of saints.

Thomas à Kempis, **Imitation of Christ,** *1473.*

kumen was der tag seins todes. Vñ da d kam.
Da rufft er zusamē seinē iungern in d stat ephe
sum .vñ daselbst macht er offenbar d3 christus
got wer.vñ das tet er mit vil offen zeychen.vnd
auch macht er offenbar daselbst das es alles

Das erst Capitel. In dem
anfang was d3 wort.vñ d3 wort w3 bey got ʒc.
Vñ wie die iūdē vō iherusalē zu iohānem sent
deten.Vñ wie iohannes ihesum sahe.ʒc.

Koberger's Ninth German Bible, 1483.

Nuremberg Chronicle, 1493.

These are hand-colored woodcuts from the Nuremberg Chronicle showing a Holocaust of the Jewish people and the incineration of books, likely Jewish texts.

BIOGRAPHY: Johannes Gutenberg (d. 1468) was a German goldsmith, inventor, printer, and publisher. His invention of movable typeset printing in the West started the Printing Revolution, which led to the democratization of reading, the wide dissemination of books and learning and changed the course of history in the West. He was the first European to use movable typeset printing circa 1439 and is credited as the inventor of the printing press that remained relatively unchanged for more than 300 years. He mass-produced movable, interlocking type, an oil-based ink, and a press patterned after the wine press. The combination of these elements facilitated an economical way to mass-produce books and offer them to the populace rather inexpensively compared to the cost of a manuscript.

Although Gutenberg published a number of tracts, indulgences, and books, his major work was his 42-line Bible published around 1454. Approximately 185 copies were printed on vellum and paper. It sold for about three years' wages. While it may seem like a lot by modern standards, this was a bargain in those days, considering that a handwritten Bible would take a single scribe minimally a year to complete and would obviously cost much more than the scribe's wage to acquire.

Gutenberg had borrowed a considerable sum of money from a lender named Johann Füst, putting up his print shop and stock as collateral. Gutenberg's lead apprentice was Peter Schöffer. Füst alleged that Gutenberg had misappropriated the funds loaned to him and foreclosed on the print shop. Füst was given half of the Bibles previously printed, took over the operation, and hired Schöffer, who later married Füst's daughter. Füst and Schöffer embarked on a profitable printing venture using Gutenberg's press. Gutenberg was able to rebound and continued printing, although the details about his later activities are unclear. Despite the setbacks and disappointments, Gutenberg's innovation has been credited as the most important development in the second millennium CE. It is also of great interest that the Bible was the first book printed in the West, revealing the desire people had to own the Bible.

CHAPTER SIX

THE REFORMATION THEATER

The Reformation Theater Exhibit Gallery

TIMELINE: The Reformation Theater is set after the publication of Desiderius Erasmus' Greek and Latin New Testament in 1516 and Martin Luther's posting of his 95 Theses in Wittenberg on 31 October 1517. The items displayed in the case just outside of the Reformation Theater represent a narrow time period ranging from a letter written by Luther in 1518, several days before facing church officials on charges of heresy, to a magnificent, oversized manuscript indulgence with illumination on vellum dating to 1525.

GEOGRAPHICAL RANGE: The items on display were produced in Italy, Germany, and England.

THE SETTING: The Reformation Theater allows visitors a front-row seat in a hypothetical, and sometimes heated, exchange between three giants in the church from the first half of the 16th century: Martin Luther, Desiderius Erasmus, and Johann Eck. Each represents a different perspective on the condition of the church.

This video docent holds an advertisement announcing an upcoming debate between Erasmus, Luther, and Eck.

Luther took confession seriously. When people stumbled into the confessional claiming they had no need for absolution because they had purchased an indulgence, he was deeply stirred; he recognized that the papacy was exploiting superstitious Germans for financial gain. Some say that Erasmus attacked the monk in his belly (criticizing the hypocritical excesses of the so-called ascetic life), and Luther got to the pope through his wallet. Others say that Erasmus laid the egg that Luther hatched. In any event, the Reformation Theater introduces some of the major issues of the early Reformation: questions of forgiveness and faith, the importance for vernacular Scripture, and the role of tradition and the pope.

Unless I am convinced by Scriptures or reason
for I do not trust either in the pope or in councils alone
I am bound by the Scriptures.
My conscience is taken captive by the Word of God.
I cannot and will not recant anything
since it is neither safe nor right to go against conscience.
May God help me, Amen.

- Martin Luther

Luther has a heavy conscience and is deeply concerned about his sin and forgiveness. He is a monk, a priest, and a scholar. In the course of his public lectures on Scripture, he obtained a copy of Erasmus' Greek and Latin New Testament published in 1516. In preparation for his lecture on

Romans 1, Luther saw that the Greek text in Erasmus' edition had a meaning completely different from the Latin text regarding the "righteousness of God." Instead of seeing God as an angry judge ready to mete out punishment at every turn in life, he realized that the Greek text indicated that God was a source of righteousness and provided a way for forgiveness and right-standing before Him. This was revolutionary for the beleaguered Luther, and he offers thanks to Erasmus.

Erasmus, a meticulous scholar, had written a satirical attack about the abuses that had developed over time in the church. His attack was honest, insightful, biting, and extremely humorous. It was called *In Praise of Folly*, and, while it was banned by the church for centuries, it amused even its leader at the time, Pope Leo X. Luther hoped to find a kindred spirit in Erasmus.

The third participant is Eck, a Dominican monk and an ardent and inflexible defender of the papacy and the church. He was Luther's nemesis, and he was not amused by Erasmus. He rejected Luther's ideas as heresy, and he warned Erasmus of the error of his ways. His dogmatic argument caused Erasmus reticently to realign himself with the church but caused Luther to compose his 95 Theses and post them on the door of Castle Church, where he ministered.

Luther, Signed Letter: Last Will and Testament, October 1518

This short letter was written the night before Luther faced charges of heresy in Augsburg just less than a year after he nailed the 95 Theses to the door of his church. It represents a unique perspective into the psyche of one of the most influential people in history during a time of utmost crisis. The letter, composed in Latin, is written by a hand that is clearly unafraid. His signature is visible at the bottom of the letter. The text was transliterated in the 19th century when the letter was mounted.

Babylonian Captivity of the Church, 1520

This radical treatise attacked the central responsibility of the Mass, the control of the clergy over the laity, the sacramental system as the means of attaining grace, and called the pope the antichrist. Luther argues the central ideas of his reform: that salvation is based on faith in the promises of God, and that all believers are priests. A Renaissance-inspired woodcut with figures and foliation surrounds the title. The use of this type of motif signaled that the book was an outgrowth of the revival of learning and promised to investigate the earliest sources. The emblem of the City of Wittenberg is at the top center. There is a heart with a cross at the bottom

and a serpent entwining the cross. It is flanked by two armed figures, one looking alarmed. Although the serpent lifted in the wilderness by Moses in the Book of Numbers is associated with Jesus, this may represent the more common association with the devil and visually indicating the thesis of the book—that the church has been uncoiled by evil. The elaborate woodcut border to the title has been hand colored.

Henry VIII's Defense of the Seven Sacraments, 1522

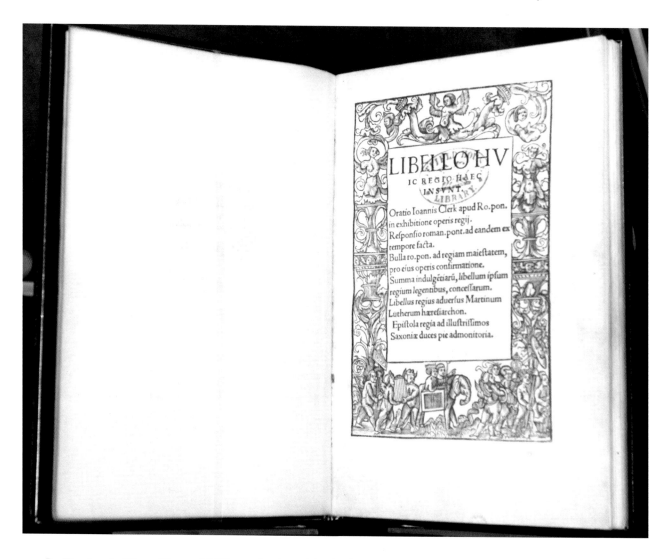

In England, King Henry VIII, no doubt with the help of Cardinal Wolsey and probably his tutor, Bishop John Fisher, wrote this rebuttal to Martin Luther's Babylonian Captivity of the Church, 1520. Henry defends the sacramental system as a means of obtaining grace and as the foundation of Catholic orthodoxy. He also defends the doctrine of transubstantiation. The pope awarded him the Golden Rose Award, as Defender of the Faith. But Henry's ideas changed with the winds of time and according to his own personal circumstances. The title is surrounded by an elaborate woodcut. Luther published a counterattack in both Latin and in German.

Leo X's *Exsurge Domine*

Pope Leo X

This is one of several editions of Pope Leo X's famous Bull (or papal decree) titled *Exsurge Domine* or Rise up, O Lord, condemning Luther. The Bull was published with supplemental materials by Andreas Lutz in 1520. The pope condemned 41 of Luther's ideas found in his writings. Surprisingly, justification by faith was not one of them. He equated Luther to a wild German boar, and even more dangerously the pope associated him with Jan Hus (sometimes spelled John Huss), who was condemned as a heretic and burned at the stake in 1415. The pope urged Luther to repent and recant within 60 days. If he refused, he would be excommunicated. What's more, all who embraced his ideas or harbored him would face execution as a heretic. All people were forbidden to read, print, or publish any of Luther's works and were commanded to burn them. Many did. Luther responded by burning the Bull. The title is surrounded by a simple architectural woodcut.

Idealized image of Luther burning the
Papal Bull Exsurge Domine *outside the walls of Wittenberg.*

BIOGRAPHY: Martin Luther (d. 1546) was raised in a devout home, the son of a stern copper miner. He joined an Augustinian monastery after he had made what he considered afterward to have been a hasty vow, dashing his parents' hopes that he would be a lawyer. He later was consecrated as a priest. Luther took his monastic vows seriously and later commented that he nearly martyred himself with his ascetic practices. He spent hours daily in confession but found no relief for his deep sense of guilt and shame for his sin. His abbot suggested a pilgrimage to Rome, hoping Luther would find relief. Instead, he observed flippant and hypocritical practices.

Luther was pursuing a doctoral degree in theology when a new university opened in Wittenberg. Luther's abbot recommended that he teach at the new university; he became priest of Castle Church in Wittenberg and professor of theology. Indulgence peddlers were selling complete pardon for all sins, certified by the pope, throughout Germany. Imagine Luther's response in the confessional when people felt no need to confess their sins to a priest who himself had felt the need to confess his sins habitually. To further the confusion, Castle Church was the repository of the largest collection of holy relics outside of Rome. Pilgrims flooded the city to view the relics in the church on All Saints' Day. Luther had been giving public lectures on Romans and had come to understand that forgiveness, peace, and a right standing before a holy God could only come by faith in the work of Christ and the promises of God in the Bible. There was not room for pardons that could be purchased or religious superstitions that had no biblical precedent.

Luther responded by nailing 95 Theses to his own church doors, willing to debate any of his suppositions. Within a few short years, hundreds of thousands of Luther's tracts were distributed in the vernacular throughout German-speaking countries. The Reformation had begun, and the political and religious boundaries of Europe would forever change. Luther wrote theological tracts, sermons, letters, commentaries, catechisms, hymns, controversial works, and a translation of the Bible that he worked on with others from the early 1520s through 1546, continuously revising and perfecting it. When asked at the end of his life which of his works he considered most important, he named his Commentary on Galatians, his work titled *Bondage of the Will*, and his translation of the Bible.

Door at Luther's Castle Church where he nailed his 95 Theses

CHAPTER SEVEN

CASTLE TOWER WITTENBERG

Castle Tower Wittenberg Exhibit Gallery

TIMELINE: The books on display in the Castle Church Tower study in Wittenberg include an Erasmus Greek and Latin New Testament published in 1516 and the Esmer (Catholic) German edition of the New Testament published in 1527.

A video docent playing a young Martin Luther struggling over questions about faith, works, and the Bible.

GEOGRAPHICAL RANGE: The items on display in the Castle Church Tower study in Wittenberg come from Spain, Switzerland, and Germany.

THE SETTING: This is Martin Luther's study in Castle Church Tower in Wittenberg where Luther had his famous revelation studying the text of Romans 1 in preparation for public lectures. It was one of his responsibilities as priest and professor of theology. He had previously lectured through the Book of Hebrews and the Book of Psalms. The text that he used for the later lectures is at the Herzog August Bibliothek in Wolfenbütel, Germany (a national repository of Luther texts, filled with notes written in his own hand). The Green Collection has an academic relationship with this German library, and a block book is there on display.

As Luther apparently pored over the recently published Erasmus Greek and Latin New Testament, he claims that his eyes were opened and an altogether new understanding of Scripture was revealed to him. He said that he understood that the phrase "righteousness of God is revealed from heaven" was not referring in the immediate context to the sense that God was a righteous judge. Rather, He was the source of righteousness (a theological and legal term indicating that a right standing had been granted) to those who had faith in the promises

The study where Martin Luther translated his New Testament.

of God. In his account of the transforming experience, Luther continued by saying that he raced through Scripture by memory, apparently comparing the Latin text with the Greek text now available to him as a result of Erasmus' revolutionary version.

The small study area consists of two cases, one containing several early German translations of Scripture. The other case contains early printed texts of the Scriptures in the original languages available to the early translators. These texts reflect the Renaissance ideal of returning to the original sources of the Judeo-Christian religion. The mantra of this era was the Latin *ad fontes*, meaning returning to the fountain or source of vitality of the present by making available and studying ancient sources and by comparing them with the present state of affairs.

> *I strongly oppose from those who would not have regular people read the Bible*
> *nor have them translated into the vernacular.*
> *I would wish that all women—girls even—would read the Gospels and Epistles.*
> *I wish that they were translated into all languages of all people.*
> *To make them understood is surely the first step.*
> *It may be that they might be ridiculed by many, but some would take them to heart.*
> *I long that the husbandman would sing them to himself as he follows the plough,*
> *That the weaver should hum them to the tune of his shuttle,*
> *And that the traveler should beguile with their stories the tedium of his journey.*
>
> - Desiderius Erasmus, *On Christianity*

Erasmus' *Novum Instrumentum Omne*, 1516

QVATVOR EVANGELIA, AD VETVSTISSI
EXEMPLARIVM LATINORVM FIDEM, E
GRAECAM VERITATEM AB ERASMO R
RODAMO SACRAE THEOLOGIAE PROF
SORE DILIGENTER RECOGNITA.

ΕΥΑΓΓΕΛΙΟΝ ΚΑΤΑ
ΜΑΤΘΑΙΟΝ.

EVANGELIVM SE
MATTHAE\

During his lifetime, Erasmus published four editions of the Greek New Testament, accompanied by a Latin text or texts. The first edition is called *Novum Instrumentum Omne*. It was published in 1516 by Johannes Froben, an illustrious publisher of Bibles and classical works and a collaborator with Erasmus, who realized that it would be incredibly popular and useful. The editorial work was rushed. Erasmus, generally remembered as a careful scholar, said that the first edition was the most precipitous work ever published. The plan was to print the New Testament prior to the completion of the more lengthy, cumbersome, and expensive multi-volume *Complutensian Polyglot* and actually secure a license for exclusive distribution—a tact that delayed the sale of the *Complutensian Polyglot* which was not widely distributed until 1521–1522. By that time, three editions of Erasmus' New Testament were in circulation and at least one independent "knock-off" edition of the work.

Erasmus used only a limited number of biblical manuscripts and never had more than one in his possession at a time. None of the manuscripts had the last verses of Revelation, forcing Erasmus to create his own text by translating the Latin Vulgate back into Greek, unintentionally introducing several grammatical errors into his version of the Greek text. But the edition and notes were an incredible success, despite papal demands that subsequent editions include 1 John 5:7, an explicit verse supporting the doctrine of the Trinity not found in any Greek manuscript of 1 John 5 or any Latin text prior to the sixth century. Erasmus had printed an independent translation of the Latin New Testament. The church demanded that a standard version of the Latin Vulgate be published in subsequent translations, although the Erasmus edition was included as a second Latin edition in later versions of the work. The book is opened to an elaborate Renaissance border at the opening of the Gospel of St. Matthew.

Luther New Testament, 1524

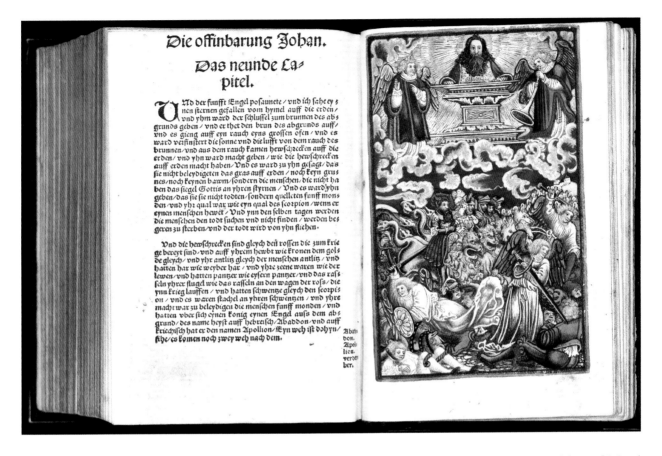

This is an extraordinarily rare and fabulously illustrated, painted, and gilded early edition of Martin Luther's famous New Testament that first appeared in 1522. The translation was done while Luther was in exile after his excommunication at the Diet of Worms. The Elector Frederick the Wise put Luther in hiding while he worked with his Wittenberg colleagues, especially the eminent Greek scholar Philip Melanchthon. The woodcut series that accompanies Revelation provides a vivid and literal perspective on the meaning of the text. The lavish, hand-painted copy by an accomplished artist was most likely commissioned by a member of the nobility close to Luther.

This is the first edition of Luther's New Testament in a smaller, more portable format. It is actually the fifth edition of Luther's widely popular translation published by Lotter, in this revised second state, showing the demand for the translation in the two years since its first appearance. Luther's New Testament represents a milestone in the history of German Bible translation and had a huge impact in the promotion of the Reformation, as well as in the dissemination of the High German language. The Bible contains 44 full-page woodcuts printed from 34 wood-blocks executed by Georg Lemberger (d. 1540), lavishly colored and heightened with gold, plus 27 larger initials and border decorations following Lucas Cranach's highly skilled illustrations of Revelation.

Luther Old Testament, Volume II, 1525

This is a volume of the first edition of Martin Luther's translation of the Old Testament, from Hebrew into German. The Old Testament appeared in sections between 1523 and 1533 (in Low German) and 1534 (in High German). The last sections to appear were the Prophets and the Old Testament Apocrypha. As with the New Testament, the printer incorporated the finest artists to illustrate the text, bring it to life, and make it appear tangible and real to the reader.

This is the second volume of the first edition of Martin Luther's translation of the Old Testament containing Joshua through Nehemiah. Elaborate initials were created throughout by Georg Lemberger. The volume contains four full-page woodcuts, including the title page and 20 half-page woodcuts by Lucas Cranach the Younger and two devices: the Lamb of God and a rose with a heart and cross flanked by the initials *M* and *L* for Martin Luther. While Luther knew Hebrew and translated from the Hebrew text, he worked in close collaboration with his academic colleagues at Wittenberg. He also consulted the LXX, the Vulgate, the work of Sebastian Münster, the *Glossa Ordinaria*, and especially the Postilla of Nicolas de Lyra as well as the Latin translation of *Sanctes Pagnini* from the Hebrew for later sections. Luther used a copy of the Hebrew text printed in Brescia in 1494 which still survives.

Emser New Testament, 1527

This edition of the German New Testament was a Catholic response to Luther's popular translation. The work was executed by Jerome (or Hieronymus) Emser, a former associate of Luther who returned to the Catholic Church and became a bitter adversary of the Reformer. The work is little more than a reworking of Luther's translation, toning down the Protestant language and attempting to conform the translation to the Latin text. Anti-Protestant notes were also incorporated throughout.

The woodcut on the facing page of the elaborate title shows Moses with the tablets of the law, King David with his harp, and St. Paul with his symbol: a sword. St. Peter stands next to the throne and a young boy timidly draws close to Jesus. Other peasant-like folks look on with interest, as they gather in front of an enthroned Virgin Mary, holding the baby Jesus who points at the spectacle. Both are surrounded by a radiant glow. They are shaded by a sprawling tree. The clouds swirl in the sky. Cherubs sit above the throne. The pope, wearing his three-tiered crown, breaks though the clouds. This is in stark contrast with woodcuts found in Luther's New Testament, in the Revelation cycle, showing God appearing in the clouds.

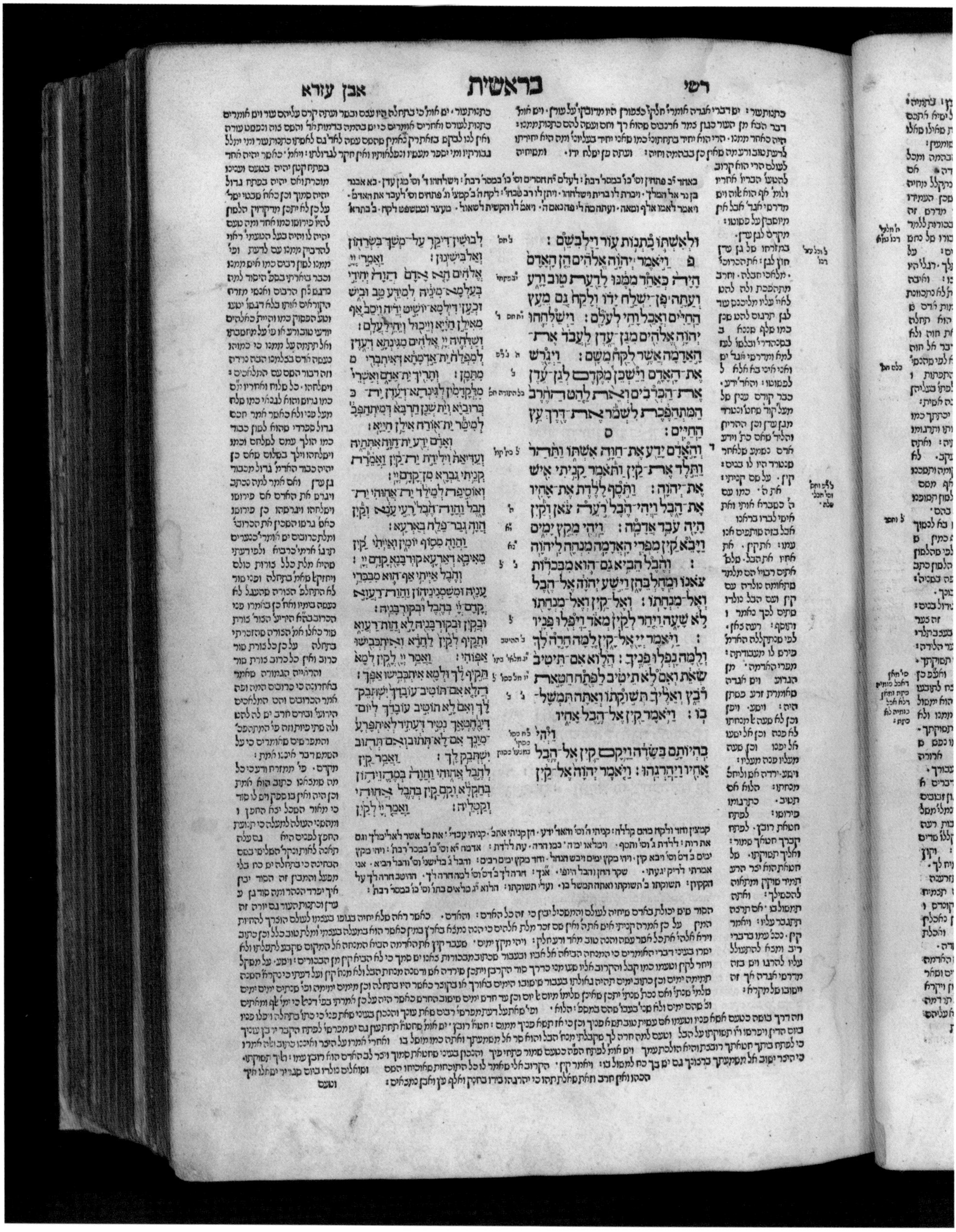

Bomberg Old Testament, 1525.

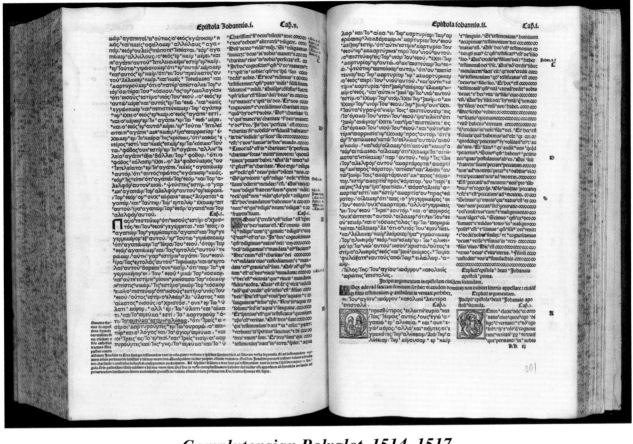

Complutensian Polyglot, 1514–1517.

Erasmus' Greek New Testament, 1521.

BIOGRAPHY: Desiderius Erasmus was the illegitimate son of a priest. He was raised in a monastery, but his scholarly disposition found him unsuitable for monastic life and he was released from his vows. He had a sharp acumen and a sharper wit. He traveled to Italy to learn Greek from refugees who had fled Constantinople after the fall of the city to the Turks. Greek at this time was no longer a banned language associated with the supposed heresy of the schismatic Eastern Church. Erasmus settled for some time in England, where he taught and enjoyed the patronage of Sir Thomas More and others.

Erasmus has been called the Prince of the Christian Humanists. *Humanist* was a term used at that time to refer to an individual who had been trained in the Liberal Arts. It was a term first coined by the classical rhetorician and statesman Cicero. Erasmus published numerous works, including letters, critical editions of classical works and church fathers, theological and practical works, a critical edition of the Greek New Testament and critical notes, his own edition of the Latin New Testament, and a paraphrase of the Latin New Testament with a commentary that formed the basis for an English translation sponsored by Henry VIII's last wife, Catherine Parr. Erasmus' biting, satirical work *Praise of Folly* lampooned traditions that had emerged in the church that manipulated the ill-informed faithful who were ruled by a personified Folly rather than the personified Wisdom found in Proverbs and noncanonical Jewish works. While even amusing the pope, the work was banned by the Inquisition for centuries. This work and his scholarly editions inadvertently supported the Protestant Reform movement. Ironically, Erasmus was a bitter opponent of Luther and remained a faithful son of the Roman Church.

CHAPTER EIGHT

ANNE BOLEYN'S THRONE ROOM AND DUNGEON

Ann Boleyn's Throne Room and Dungeon Exhibit Gallery

TIMELINE: The books associated with Anne Boleyn's Throne Room and Dungeon range in date from a printing of an anonymous treatise *Why Scripture Should Be in English* (facsimile edition), originally composed in the early 15th century and printed in 1530. Earlier first editions of Tyndale's works date from 1528. The later works published by Sir Thomas More date to 1534, one with an indulgence for an Irish priest—found in the cover that dates to 1574.

GEOGRAPHICAL RANGE: The items on display in Anne Boleyn's Throne Room and Dungeon were printed in Germany, the Netherlands, and England.

THE SETTING: Martin Luther's early reform stirred rumbles of protest in England. While Reformation in Germany and elsewhere on the Continent (often referred to as Continental Reform) was similar in many respects to reform in England (often referred to as Insular Reform), there were some very important distinctions that affected the timing, implementation, and even the nature of the reform of the church in England. One of the major distinctions was that Insular Reform was more politically driven and controlled than was Continental Reform, despite Luther's *Appeal to the German Nobility to Reform the Church* published in 1520. This provides a backdrop for Anne Boleyn's Throne Room and Dungeon.

You have probably heard the expression of someone going from "rags to riches." This room tells the opposite story with the life, activity, and death of Queen Anne Boleyn, Henry VIII's second wife. The story is revealed in two parts. The first part is told by Queen Anne sitting regally on her throne, living what she called "the happiest life ever." Little did she know how short lived that would be and the fate that awaited her. The second part is told by Anne in prison awaiting her execution.

Anne explains that the annulment of Henry's first marriage from Catherine of Aragon led to a separation between the church in England and the church in Rome. Henry eventually married Anne, the chambermaid to the former queen. Anne surrounded herself with Protestant advisors, many of whom were friends of William Tyndale. She supported the Reform and quietly promoted the early works of Tyndale, one of which called for the king to rule the church in his land. But another claimed that Henry's divorce of Catherine was due to the manipulation of the cardinal in England, which enraged the king. Turbulent waters were ahead.

Anne reigned a short time. The focus moves from her throne room to the dungeon. She kneels on the cold stone floor, lying in the lap of her own chambermaid. How quickly the tides of fortune change. Her chambermaid cannot contain her deep distress. Weak, Anne can barely raise her head to tell her fate. She has been condemned to death on fabricated charges of immorality. The fact of the matter is that King Henry desperately wanted a male heir to succeed him. Anne had given birth to a beautiful daughter named Elizabeth but had miscarried a baby boy. Her support of Tyndale and the Reformation also led to her downfall.

Fewer than ten copies of Tyndale's second edition of his New Testament published in 1534 survive. One belonged to Anne Boleyn, bearing her Coat of Arms—evidence that she studied it. She turns her head mournfully to the onlookers, peering with disbelief into her jail cell. With a faint voice, she tells them that as Tyndale's Scriptures have taught her how to live, they will also teach her how to die. Clinging to the hope of the promise of life after death, Anne was said to have carried her copy of Tyndale's New Testament to the chopping block at the Tower of London.

A Lady-in-Waiting in the court of Queen Anne Boleyn describes court protocol and intimates of the queen's impending doom.

I defy the Pope and all his laws
If God spares my life
I will make a ploughboy know more of the Scripture than you do!

- William Tyndale

Alone in prison strong
I wait my destiny.
Woe worth this cruel hap that I
should taste this misery!
Toll on, thou passing bell;
Ring out my doleful knell;
Let thy sound my death tell.
Death doth draw nigh;
there is no remedy.

- Queen Anne Boleyn, a stanza from "Oh Death, Rock Me Asleep"

Anonymous, *Why Scripture Should Be in English*, 1530 facsimile

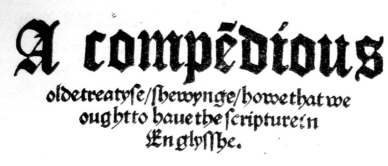

A compēdious oldetreatyse/shewynge/howe that we ought to haue the scripture in Englysshe.

❧The excusacyon of ẏ treatyse

Though I am olde/clothed ī barbarous wede
Nothynge garnysshed with gaye eloquency
Yet I tell the trouth/yf ye lyst to take hede
Agaynst theyr frowarde/furious frenesy
Which recken it for a great heresy
And vnto laye people greuous outrage
To haue goddes worde in their natyfe langage

Enemyes I shall haue/many a shoren crowne
With forked cappes and gaye croosys of golde
Which to maynteyne ther ambicious renowne
Are glad laye people in ignorance to holde
Yet to shewe the verite/one maye be bolde
All though it be a prouerbe daylye spoken
Who that tellyth trouth/his head shalbe broke.

❧Vnto the Reader.

Grace ād peace: not that ẏ worlde ge-
uyth/but from god the father ꝗ oure
sauioure Jesu Chrift with increace of
the holy spryt be with the and all that thurste
ẏ truthe. Amē. ❧Cōsyderynge ẏ malyciousnes

This is a fascinating photo-lithographic facsimile of the only surviving trace of two treatises. One called *Compendous Olde Treatyse* (or *Why Scripture Should Be in English*) likely dated to the days of the persecution of the followers of Wycliffe. It calls for the king to permit the dissemination of Scripture in English. The tract was clearly edited at a later date, referring to Tyndale. The editor introduced the work with the poem that makes interesting contrasts. While the vernacular language lacks the eloquence of Latin, it can speak to a layperson's heart. The editor also speaks of how the people are grieved by the suppression of God's Word and of how those who favor the vernacular Scripture in English can expect to face retribution.

Tyndale, *Obedience of the Christian Man*, 1528

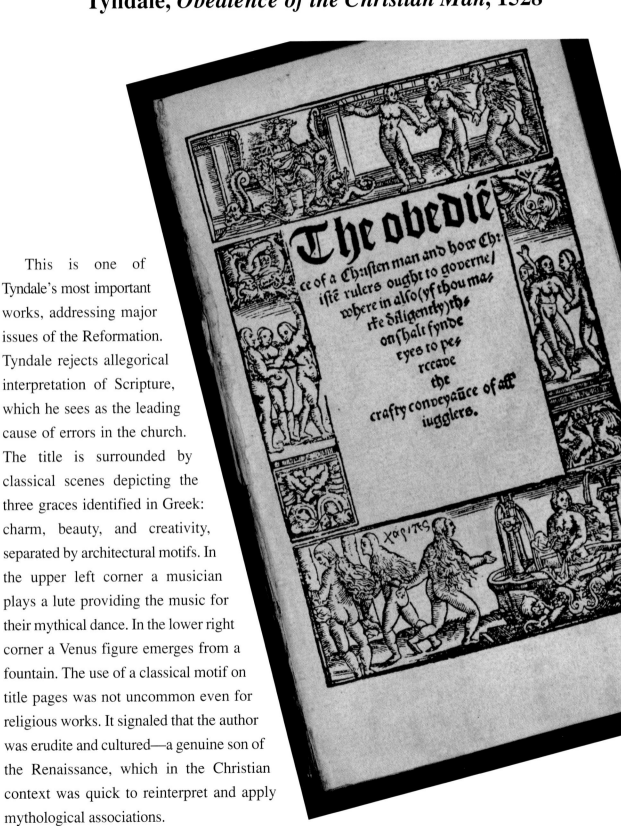

This is one of Tyndale's most important works, addressing major issues of the Reformation. Tyndale rejects allegorical interpretation of Scripture, which he sees as the leading cause of errors in the church. The title is surrounded by classical scenes depicting the three graces identified in Greek: charm, beauty, and creativity, separated by architectural motifs. In the upper left corner a musician plays a lute providing the music for their mythical dance. In the lower right corner a Venus figure emerges from a fountain. The use of a classical motif on title pages was not uncommon even for religious works. It signaled that the author was erudite and cultured—a genuine son of the Renaissance, which in the Christian context was quick to reinterpret and apply mythological associations.

Tyndale, *Practice of Prelates*, 1530

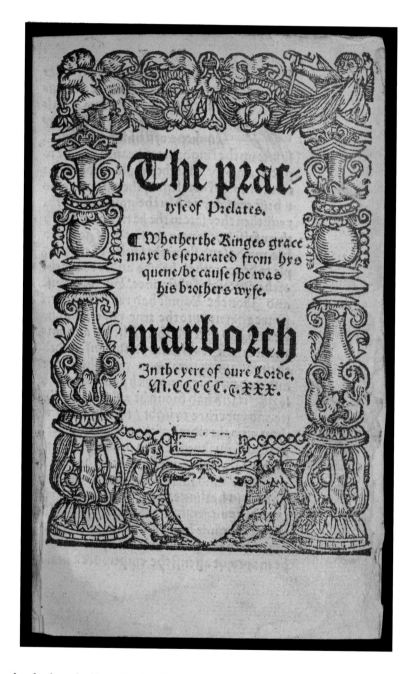

This invective single-handedly attacks the corrupt power of the church and King Henry VIII's justification for his divorce of Catherine of Aragon. Tyndale places the blame directly on the machinations of the English Cardinal Wolsey; in doing so, he not only condemns the unjustified premise for the divorce but also rejects the legitimacy of the second marriage to Anne Boleyn. Ironically Anne would become a supporter of Tyndale, surrounding herself with Protestant advisors, which ultimately led to her own demise. The title page is surrounded by a fanciful Renaissance architectural motif.

Tyndale, *On Wicked Mammon*, (1528) 1536

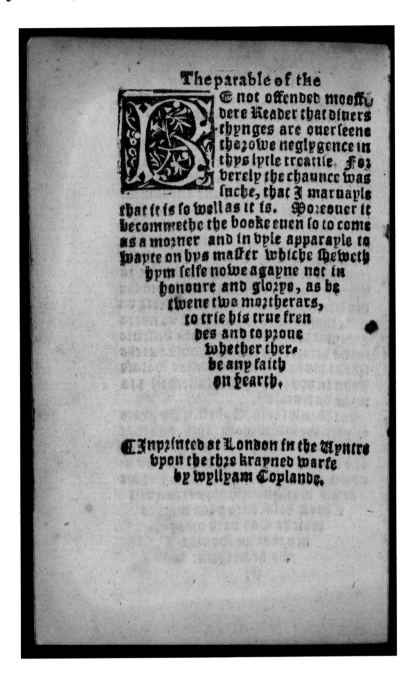

This is William Tyndale's publication of a sermon by Luther followed by a short theological treatise on one of the core issues of the Protestant Reformation: the relationship between the doctrine of justification by faith and that of good works. The short book opens with a six-line capital letter. The printer's colophon is at the bottom of the page. This was a particularly dangerous time to print a work by Tyndale, especially in London. The final words are a fitting epitaph, considering the timing of this particular publication in relationship to the recent execution of Tyndale.

The Wives of Henry VIII

King Henry VIII,
by Hans Holbein the Younger.

Queen Catherine of Aragon.

Thomas Cranmer, archbishop of Canterbury.

Cranmer's execution as depicted in Foxe's **Book of Martyrs.**

BIOGRAPHY: Anne Boleyn (d. 1536) was queen of England from 1533 to 1536 as the second wife of King Henry VIII. Anne was a commoner, educated and trained in Belgium and France and eventually became maid of honor to Queen Catherine of Aragon, Henry's first wife. She refused to follow in her sister's footsteps and become the king's mistress, hoping instead for the annulment of his marriage to Catherine, which would make for the promise of a legitimate marriage as well as the crown. Pope Clement VII refused to annul the marriage, so Cardinal Thomas Wolsey, archbishop of York and chief advisor to the king, was dismissed. The Boleyns' chaplain, Thomas Cranmer, was eventually appointed archbishop of Canterbury. Henry married Anne in 1533. Cranmer then declared Henry's first marriage null and void, and the second marriage, legitimate. The pope excommunicated Henry and Cranmer, resulting in a break between the Church of England and the Church of Rome. Shortly thereafter, Anne gave birth to Elizabeth but never to the son and male successor Henry desired to have.

Anne surrounded herself with Protestant advisors, friends of William Tyndale. It is believed that she promoted Tyndale's book titled *Obedience of the Christian Man* to support Henry's taking control of the Church of England. A second edition of Tyndale's New Testament, printed in 1534, was owned and cherished by Anne. Her personal copy, bearing her coat of arms and containing her personal notes, is preserved in the British Library. It was a condemned book owned by a condemned queen. Her zealous support of Protestant reform may, in part, have led to her demise. Other charges were brought against her, and she was tried and condemned to death. It is said that she carried her copy of Tyndale's New Testament to her death in 1536.

CHAPTER NINE

TYNDALE'S EXECUTION

Tyndale's Execution Exhibit Gallery

TIMELINE: The books associated with Tyndale's Execution range in date from a facsimile of his first printed fragment of the Gospel of St. Matthew in 1525 through the publication of Tyndale's *An Exposition upon the V, VI, VII Chapters of Matthew,* 1550 or 1549.

GEOGRAPHICAL RANGE: The items on display associated with Tyndale's execution were published in Germany, the Netherlands, and England.

THE SETTING: Inspired by the woodcut illustrating the execution of Tyndale in 1536 in Foxe's *Book of Martyrs.* The setting is in Belgium. William Tyndale had been betrayed to the authorities, tried as a heretic, found guilty, and condemned to death. Scholars were given the dignity, if you can call it that, of being strangled to death. Then the corpse was incinerated. As one enters the dungeon, one can peer out through the bars of the jail cell and see Tyndale tied to the stake. The crowd jeers insults at him, and a rope is tied around his neck. The executioner gruffly tells him to speak his last words, to make his peace with God, and to get on with it quickly.

Tyndale looks over the mob, unafraid. He stares through the jail cell with steely eyes and speaks boldly to the onlookers. Without any malice, he says he has been condemned, chiefly for his tireless efforts to translate and publish the Scriptures into English. He encourages the crowd to read the Words of Life that he has given his life to translate and for which he now will pay the ultimate price, his actions deemed criminal.

His eyes scour the crowd and look into the distance, as if to heaven. He draws a deep breath and hangs his head, choking on his words. The executioner barks at Tyndale to be done with it. With a last surge of energy, Tyndale lifts his head and eyes to the mob and cries out his last prayer to God: not to forgive his sin, ease his pain, make his end swift, receive his soul, comfort his loved ones, give him grace to endure or even a way of deliverance. He doesn't recant or retract what he has done with the hope of mercy. No, the last burden on his heart is for God to open the king of England's eyes to allow the people to have the Bible in English. The lights dim. Tyndale dies, and his dying prayer was answered.

But the onlooker is left with haunting questions about justice and the ultimate sacrifice that people like Tyndale made to preserve the Bible in the vernacular taken for granted in a modern age where freedom can result in carelessness.

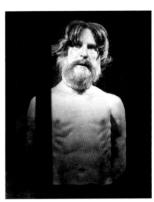

*The clergy of the English Church should have provided
light to the people but they kept them from the knowledge of the Bible
which they would not translate or let others translate
keeping people in darkness just like Tyndale said.*

- Foxe's *Book of Martyrs*

William Tyndale at the stake

Tyndale, Gospel of St. Matthew Fragment, 1525 facsimile

This is an exact facsimile of the first attempt to print the Scriptures independently in English by William Tyndale in 1525. The work was disrupted by a Catholic antagonist who had previously condemned the notion of the laity reading Scripture. The full-page woodcut depicts St. Matthew and an angel on a page preceding the Gospel. St. Matthew is seated at a writing desk with a quill in his hand. The angel holds an inkpot and the Evangelist has dipped his quill and is ready to write. The two are surrounded by pillars, as if in a monastic scriptorium adjacent to a cloister. Vines and tendrils connect the tops of the pillars and a winged putto looks down from the clouds in the center, as if curious. There is a mountainous landscape in the background and a distant city on a hill, which might be an allusion to the Gospel, as well.

Tyndale, New Testament, 1526 facsimile

This is an exact facsimile of William Tyndale's first edition of the New Testament printed in English in 1526, lacking only the general title and contents. It is one of three known. The rest were condemned to the flames. It is opened to the beginning of the Gospel of St. John. The Evangelist wears a long scarlet robe, sits on the grass, and looks at figures in the background as he writes in a book. Typically the images of the Evangelist were dedicated to a page preceding the Gospel. This marks a departure and what would appear to be an emphasis on the message of the pure Gospel.

Tyndale, Pentateuch, 1530

This book is a monumental achievement in English Bible translation with a lasting legacy. It is the first edition of the English translation of the Pentateuch (the five Books of Moses). The translation was vigorously repressed. It is exceedingly rare with only eight known copies surviving, but the translation is alive and well in every later English translation of the Pentateuch. The photo shows one of the 11 full-page woodcuts in the book, all from the Book of Exodus. The images are based on woodcuts by Hans Holbein. The woodcut shows the ornaments of the Tabernacle from a unique perspective. The coverings of the Tabernacle have been pulled back for the reader to look inside to see the furnishings. The quaint surroundings, including the Tudor house, are all mindful of the contemporary setting.

Tyndale, New Testament, 1535? (An undocumented edition)

This is an undocumented large fragment of Tyndale's New Testament dating just prior to his execution. Tyndale fully understood the high calling of translating the Scriptures correctly and effectively. Never content, this meant constant work and revision, even to his death. This fragment is the sole surviving evidence of the last revision presumably done under his direction. The text is open to the first chapter of the Book of Titus. The note states the word *bishop* is interchangeable with the word *elder*, citing a cross-reference in 1 Timothy. He goes on to describe the responsibility of the elder over the congregation, avoiding the term *church*. The definition of these terms was central to questions raised by the Protestants concerning the function of the clergy and the church.

An engraving depicting Tyndale busily translating Scripture in the dungeon prior to his execution.

Of the Churche. 519

at that tyme about xii. oz xiii. weakes, so he taried not the commyng agayne of the messenger, but in a nyghte by a meane he conueyed hym selfe. And so by Gods helpe at the openyng of the towne gate in the mornyng gatt away. And whē it was perceyued that he was gone, there was horse sent out after hym, but by the meanes that he knewe well the contrey escaped and came into Englande. But what moze trouble folowed to Poyntz of the same, it serueth not foz this place to rehearse. Maister Tyndall styll remayning in pzyson, was proffered an Aduocate and a Procurour, foz in any cryme there, it shall be permitted to counsell to make aunswere in the lawe, the whiche he refused to haue anye, but sayde, he would make aunswere foz hym selfe, and did. But it is to be thought his aunswere wyl not be put foz th, notwithstandyng he had so preached to them there who hadde hym in charge, and suche as was they conuersaunt with him in the Castel, that they repozted of hym, that if he were not a good Christian man, they knew not whom they myght take to be one.

The description and manner of the burning of
Maister Wylliam Tyndall.

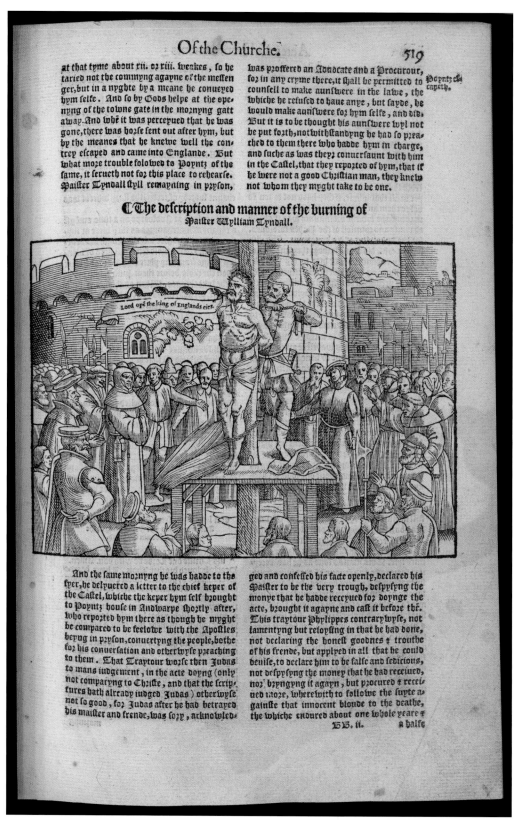

And the same mornyng he was hadde to the fyer, he delyuered a letter to the chief keper of the Castel, whiche the keper hym self bzought to Poyntz house in Andwarpe shoztly after, who repozted hym there as though he myght be compared to be feelowe with the Apostles beyng in pzyson, conuertyng the people, bothe foz his conuersation and otherwyse pzeaching to them. That Traytour wozse then Iudas to mans iudgement, in the acte doyng (only not comparyng to Chzist, and that the scriptures hath already iudged Iudas) otherwyse not so good, foz Iudas after he had betrayed his maister and frende, was sozy, acknowledged and confessed his facte openly, declared his Maister to be the very trough, despysyng the monye that he hadde receyued foz doynge the acte, bzought it agayne and cast it befoze thē. This traytour Phylippes contrarywyse, not lamentyng but reioysing in that he had done, not declaring the honest goodnes & trouthe of his frende, but applyed in all that he could deuise, to declare him to be false and sedicious, not despysyng the money that he had receiued, noz bzyngyng it agayn, but procured & receiued moze, wherewith to followe the suyte agaynste that innocent blonde to the deathe, the whiche endured about one whole yeare & a halfe

BB. ii.

Foxe's **Book of Martyrs,** *1563.*

Thomas More's manuscript on the Eucharist.

BIOGRAPHY: William Tyndale (d. 1536) was a scholar, theologian, and translator whose biblical translations have had a more profound influence on the English language than any other writer before or after. Tyndale received a BA and MA from Oxford and then studied at Cambridge for four years and later at the University of Wittenberg with Luther for a year. A gifted linguist, he was also conversant in French, Spanish, Italian, and German and fluent for his day in Greek, Hebrew, and Latin—an extraordinary achievement at the time. Tyndale served briefly as chaplain to the house of Sir John Walsh at Little Sodbury and tutor to his children but was dismissed for harboring radical religious sentiments, no doubt Luther's notions of reform. He was denied permission to publish an English translation of the Bible. Tyndale was supported by a cloth merchant named Humphrey Monmouth while he occupied his time preaching and working on a translation of the New Testament in English. In 1524 he traveled to the Continent to publish his New Testament and was assisted by an Observant Friar named William Roy.

Tyndale made his first attempt to publish the New Testament in Cologne with the printer Peter Quentell in 1525. The work was abruptly stopped. All that survives is a single copy of a portion of the Gospel of St. Matthew. Tyndale published a full edition of his New Testament in 1526 in Worms with the printer Peter Schöffer. Copies were also printed in Antwerp. The book was smuggled into England through Scotland in bales of cloth, which is where the expression "man of the cloth" originated to describe a minister. The translation was almost immediately condemned, and copies were burned in public. Only three copies of the 1526 edition survive. Contemporary accounts indicate that the spectacle of the Scriptures being burned created a great outcry. Cardinal Wolsey denounced Tyndale as a heretic. Undaunted, Tyndale published a number of theological tracts and translated and published the Pentateuch in 1530 and Jonah in 1531. He continued to revise his New Testament (1534) and worked translating other portions of the Old Testament.

Tyndale was betrayed by Henry Phillips in Antwerp in 1535. He was tried for heresy in 1536 and condemned to death. He was strangled, and his corpse was burned. His final words were "Lord! Open the king of England's eyes." And He did. Furthermore, Tyndale's work lived on influencing every later English translation of Scripture. One estimate suggests that 83 percent of the King James New Testament is taken directly from Tyndale's translation and 76 percent of the King James Old Testament. As a translator, Tyndale had an uncanny sense for the voice of the people and maintained a sense of rhythm and majesty while remaining faithful to the literal meaning of the original, given the exigencies that constrained his work.

CHAPTER TEN

KNOX'S GENEVA CHAPEL

Knox's Geneva Chapel Exhibit Gallery

TIMELINE: The books associated with Knox's Geneva Chapel date from the first edition of the Coverdale Bible published in 1535 to Hugh Broughton's *Daniel, His Chaldie Visions* published in 1596. They represent the major biblical works dating from the later reign of King Henry VIII through the reign of Queen Elizabeth I.

GEOGRAPHICAL RANGE: The items on display from Knox's Geneva Chapel were published in England, France, Brussels, and Switzerland.

THE SETTING: John Knox was a fiery Scottish preacher who fled with other Protestants to the Continent during the reign of Queen Mary Tudor I, who ascended to the throne in 1553. She sought to restore Catholicism in England with a vengeance. Knox served as a minister to the refugees for a short time in Frankfurt, Germany, and later in Geneva, Switzerland. Visitors have entered the New Church of Our Mother Mary. Knox opts not to preach another sermon on Reformed theology (a favorite theme) but chooses instead to give an overview of the amazing efforts that have been made since Tyndale to translate the Bible into English. He will survey the work over the decades, and the items he discusses are on display in the church.

In particular, Knox will mention a new translation of the Bible into English undertaken by his colleagues. The Bible was called the Geneva Bible and first appeared in 1560. It was published in more than 150 separate editions. This Bible is filled with study helps including foldout maps, prologues and theological notes, and, for the first time in an English translation, verse numbers. Knox is obviously proud of the achievements made by his friends.

An animatronic John Knox stands in the pulpit and delivers an exposition on the early history of the English Bible.

Guests should remember that they are in a church. Remove your hat, if you are wearing one, and sit down in the pew when the minister rises to preach. Also keep your wallet handy, in case they decide to take an offering!

Because the Bible is the light to our path
the key to the kingdom of heaven
our comfort in affliction
our shield and sword against evil
the source of all wisdom
the mirror where we see God's face
the record of His favor
and the only food and nourishment for our souls
we thought that we should dedicate our efforts
and study to nothing that could be more acceptable to God
and beneficial to His Church
than translating of the Bible into English

- Geneva Bible, Preface, 1560 (Revised)

An usher in Knox's Chapel describes the order of service and items on display

Geneva Bible, 1560

This is the first edition of the Bible in English produced by the Protestants in exile in Geneva during the reign of Queen Mary Tudor I and published in 1560, three years before the ascension of her half-sister, Elizabeth. This Bible was extremely popular and went through many editions. It was popular with the Puritans, in some measure because of the extensive theological notes and study support aids. The King James Bible was produced in part to counteract the popularity of this version. This was the Bible most frequently quoted by Shakespeare and Bunyan and was brought to the New World by the earliest Puritan colonists. This Bible is open to the beginning of the Gospel of St. Matthew. Preceding the first page of the Gospel is one of several full-page, foldout maps. This one shows Palestine in New Testament times.

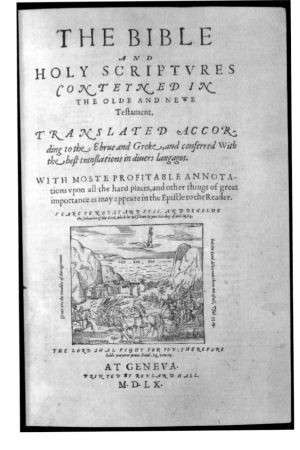

Coverdale Bible, 1535

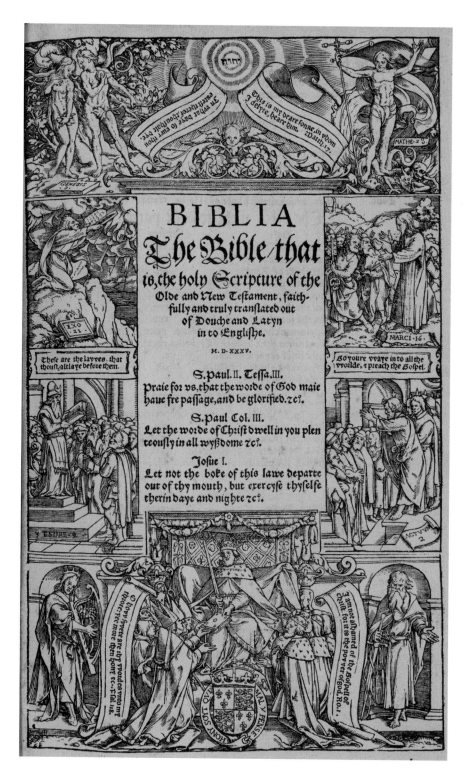

This book is a monumental achievement in English Bible translation with a lasting legacy. It is the first edition of the English translation of the Pentateuch (the five Books of Moses). The translation was vigorously repressed. It is exceedingly rare with only eight known copies surviving, but the translation is alive and well in every later English translation of the Pentateuch. The photo shows one of the 11 full-page woodcuts in the book, all from the Book of Exodus. The images are based on woodcuts by Hans Holbein. The woodcut shows the ornaments of the Tabernacle from a unique perspective. The coverings of the Tabernacle have been pulled back for the reader to look inside to see the furnishings. The quaint surroundings, including the Tudor house, are all mindful of the contemporary setting.

Matthew's Bible, 1537

This is the first translation of the entire Bible into English primarily from Hebrew, Aramaic, and Greek, incorporating translations by Tyndale. It is also the first English Bible distributed under a royal license. Thomas Matthew was probably a pseudonym for Tyndale's associate John Rogers. The Bible is open to the New Testament title page. Title pages take on great theological and later political themes of importance. The ensemble of woodcuts vividly depicts Luther's teaching about the law and the gospel, first illustrated on the general title page of the Coverdale Bible. The woodcut was executed by Lucas Cranach. Along the left border at the top, God gives the law to Moses. Under the law and dominating the left panel, the Edenic fall is depicted; on the bottom left, a corpse lays on a tomb. At the top right angels fill the sky while one carries a cross to a Mary-like figure kneeling with eyes toward heaven in the radiance of

God's blessings. The crucified Christ dominates the side panel on the right. The Lamb of God stands at the foot of the cross. On the bottom right, the risen Christ climbs from a tomb and puts an end to death. At the bottom in the middle, St. Peter and St. Paul expound the gospel to a potential convert. St. Peter holds a Bible, and both apostles point to the cross and the resurrection.

Great Bible, 1539

This is only the second English translation to receive official approval from the king, precipitated to a large degree by the popularity of unauthorized translations of the Bible and the need to provide a moderate alternative to those editions. The Bible was required to be placed in churches and read publicly and was printed in a large format to facilitate its public reading. The Bible is open to the general title page featuring a large woodcut, printed in black with red text. It depicts a powerful scene of religious propaganda. King Henry VIII sits enthroned as if in the heavens. He presents the new translation to Cranmer, to the king's right, who distributes the Bible to clergy and to Sir Thomas Cromwell, at the king's left, who distributes the Bible to the nobility. They distribute the Bible to the English people, who shout, *"Vivat Rex"* (long live the king). A single voice in the crowd calls out in the vernacular, "God save the kynge." Men, women, and children from all classes can be seen in the throng below. A minister proclaims 1 Timothy 2. God looks down from heaven on the English king and proclaims from Acts 13:22, "I have found a man after My own heart, who shall perform all My desire."

Hans Holbein the Younger, images of the Old Testament, 1549.

Bishops' Bible, 1568.

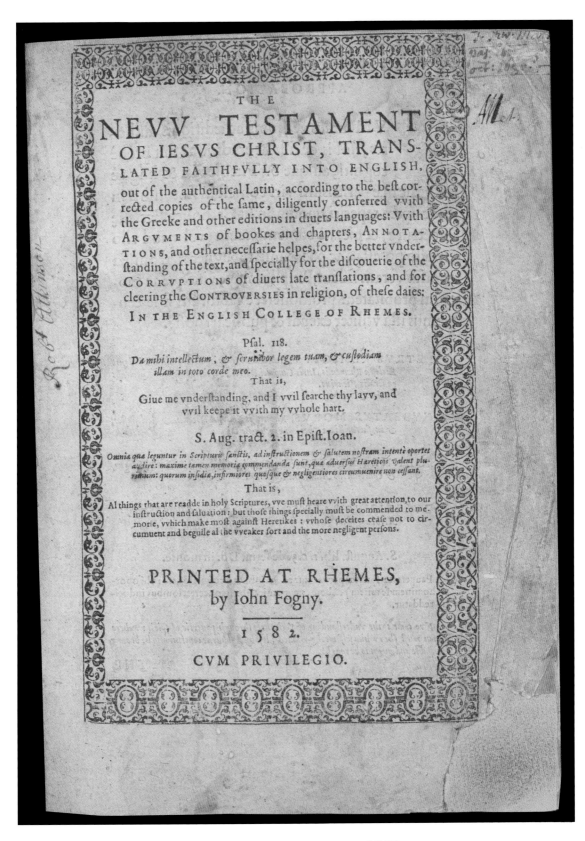

THE

NEVV TESTAMENT

OF IESVS CHRIST, TRANS-
LATED FAITHFVLLY INTO ENGLISH,

out of the authentical Latin, according to the best corrected copies of the same, diligently conferred vvith
the Greeke and other editions in diuers languages: Vvith
ARGVMENTS of bookes and chapters, ANNOTA-
TIONS, and other necessarie helpes, for the better vnderstanding of the text, and specially for the discouerie of the
CORRVPTIONS of diuers late translations, and for
cleering the CONTROVERSIES in religion, of these daies:

IN THE ENGLISH COLLEGE OF RHEMES.

Psal. 118.

*Da mihi intellectum, & scrutabor legem tuam, & custodiam
illam in toto corde meo.*

That is,

Giue me vnderstanding, and I vvil searche thy layv, and
vvil keepe it vvith my vvhole hart.

S. Aug. tract. 2. in Epist. Ioan.

*Omnia quæ leguntur in Scripturis sanctis, ad instructionem & salutem nostram intentè oportet
audire: maxime tamen memoriæ commendanda sunt, quæ aduersus Hæreticos valent plu-
rimum: quorum insidiæ, infirmiores quosque & negligentiores circumuenire non cessant.*

That is,

Al things that are readde in holy Scriptures, vve must heare vvith great attention, to our
instruction and saluation: but those things specially must be commended to me-
morie, vvhich make most against Heretikes: vvhose deceites cease not to cir-
cumuent and beguile al the vveaker sort and the more negligent persons.

PRINTED AT RHEMES,
by Iohn Fogny.

1582.

CVM PRIVILEGIO.

Rhemes New Testament, 1582.

Lord receiue my spirite.

A woodcut from Foxe's Book of Martyrs depicts the execution of John Rogers.

BIOGRAPHY: John Rogers (d. 1555) was a clergyman, Bible translator and commentator, and the first English Protestant martyr under Queen Mary Tudor I. He was educated at Cambridge. In 1534 he became the chaplain to the English merchants in Antwerp, where he met William Tyndale and was influenced by him to join the Protestant Reform movement. The two worked together on the Bible translation into English. After Tyndale's execution, Rogers continued to publish the Old Testament in English, using what was available from Tyndale and other associates including Myles Coverdale's translation of the Old Testament Apocrypha. He also relied on the Latin translation of the Hebrew Bible by Sebastian Münster, published in 1534 and 1535. Rogers probably translated only the Prayer of Manasses and the Apocryphal Song of Manasses. The complete English Bible was published in 1537 under the pseudonym of Thomas Matthew, a name previously used by William Tyndale. There were 1,500 copies printed in Paris and Antwerp. Archbishop Cranmer secured the "king's most gracious license," which had been granted to the reprint of Myles Coverdale's Bible earlier the same year. Rogers's edition of the Bible had a significant influence on the translators of the Great Bible (1539), the Bishops' Bible (1568), and the King James Version (1611).

Rogers spent time at the University of Wittenberg, where he developed a friendship with the scholar Philip Melanchthon. He later became lecturer of theology at St. Paul's in London. When Mary Tudor became queen, he preached a sermon at Paul's Cross affirming the Protestant developments in King Edward VI's reign and warning about the "pestilent popery, idolatry, and superstition." He was put under house arrest. In December 1554, Parliament re-enacted the penal statutes against Lollards (the followers of Wycliffe), and two days after the laws took effect Rogers was condemned to die at the stake. The woodcut illustration from Foxe's *Book of Martyrs* depicts Rogers's martyrdom.

CHAPTER ELEVEN

THE JERUSALEM CHAMBER

The Jerusalem Chamber Exhibit Gallery

TIMELINE: The books associated with the Jerusalem Chamber date from Sancte Pagnini's legendary Latin translation of the Bible from the Hebrew, Aramaic, and Greek published in 1528, to a small two-volume edition of the King James Bible dating to 1695.

GEOGRAPHICAL RANGE: The items on display in the Jerusalem Chamber were printed in Italy, the Netherlands, Germany, Switzerland, and England.

THE SETTING: In 1604 King James I convened scholars and ministers to Hampton Court at the urging of the Puritans to try to resolve the conflict between the zealot Puritans who read the Geneva Bible and the more moderate Protestants who read the Great Bible. Fifty-four of the most capable scholars in England convened to create a new translation. They were assigned to three committees and given simple guidelines to follow. The work was directed by Lancelot Andrewes. The 1602 edition of the Great Bible was used as a base text. They were asked to find the best translations and compare them with the most reliable critical texts of the Scriptures in the original languages. They were told to avoid the use of notes unless they were used to explain the language of the original text. They were also directed to avoid divisive translations of ecclesiastical terms. The translation took seven years.

The New Testament committee met for their final revisions at the Jerusalem Chamber, a room in Westminster Abbey. This room is a reproduction of the Jerusalem Chamber. Identical tapestries flank a reproduction of the fireplace. A portrait of King James I is on the opposite wall. A table in the center of the room has sources used by the committee strewn across the table.

Listen closely to hear the ghosts of translators debating how the Greek term *ecclesia* (εκκλησία) should be translated into English. This was a very controversial term. It was rendered *congregation* by Tyndale, *assembly* by others, but most commonly *church*. The ghosts talk about the pros and cons of the various translations. It shows that a fine line separates translation from commentary, interpretation, and theological perspective. The translation process dragged on longer than King James expected. Tempers were short, because the stakes were high. But King James was specific about how this term should be rendered, especially in light of the fact that he had been involved in previous translations. The rancor is interrupted by none other than King James, who keeps a watchful eye on the work and tells them how to translate a Greek term he cannot even pronounce properly!

Ironically, while the New Testament translators followed the translation of William Tyndale 83 percent of the time, they translated *ecclesia* as *church* by order of the king, deliberately avoiding the translation of Tyndale. Nevertheless, the translators succeeded in producing the most printed, most read, most quoted, and most influential English translation of the Bible.

We never condemned the work of previous translators
because we recognize that God used them.
They deserve to be celebrated
remembering nothing is begun and perfected at once.
We build on the foundation of those before us.
Being helped by their labor,
we work to improve their good work.
But we are not to be disdained.
We are assured if the earlier translators were alive
they would thank us.

- Preface to the King James Bible, HE edition, 1611 (Revised)

A Beefeater at his post warns of suspicious
activities in the Jerusalem Chamber, where
the New Testament translators of King
James Bible met.

1611 HE King James Version

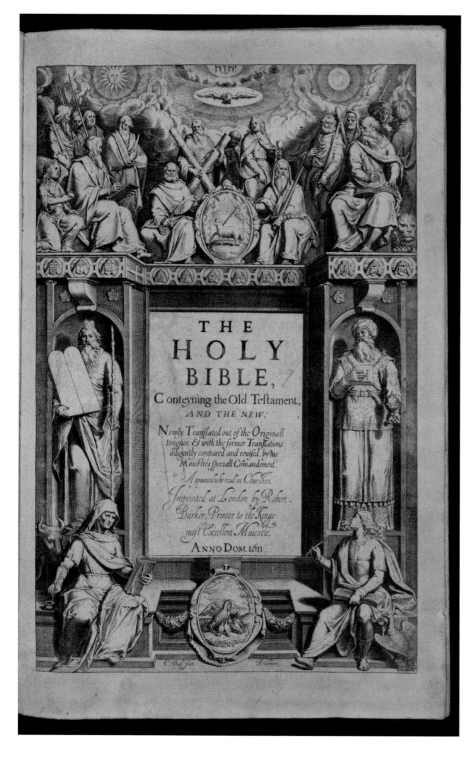

This is the best-selling, most quoted, and, arguably, the most influential book of all times. The King James Bible was not an immediate best seller. It took a number of years to overtake the extremely popular and influential Geneva Bible. Over 80 percent of the translation agrees with the translation of Tyndale, who must be credited for the directness of the translation and majesty of the language. The Bible is open to the iconographic general title page beautifully crafted from a large copperplate engraving by the artist Cornelius Boel. It depicts the apostles Peter and Paul seated above the central text, which is flanked by Moses and Aaron. In the four corners sit Matthew, Mark, Luke, and John, authors of the four Gospels, with their representational animals. The other apostles stand around St. Peter and St. Paul. At the very top is the Tetragrammaton representing the name of God, YHWH (הוהי). The HE appellation of the edition refers to a particular pronoun in Ruth 3:15.

1611 HE King James Version New Testament

This is the first separately printed edition of the New Testament in the King James Version, printed the same year as the great folio 'HE' Bible, 1611. Unlike the huge folio edition of the entire Bible, this was intended to be an inexpensive edition for common use. The edition is extremely scarce due to its extensive use. The edition also contains the Psalms for use in church and for devotional purposes. The New Testament is open to the engraved title page. Angels surround the Tetragrammaton (הוהי) in the clouds above. The title of the volume is surrounded by an architectural motif of columns topped with kneeling, praying figures looking into the heavens. An altar is placed between the columns and above the title. Incense emanates from a pot shaped like a heart to represent prayers to God. Beneath the title a crowned King David kneels and looks into heaven as he plays his harp. He sings a verse from Psalm 51 in Latin: *"Cor mundum crea in me Deus"* or "Create in me a clean heart, O God!"

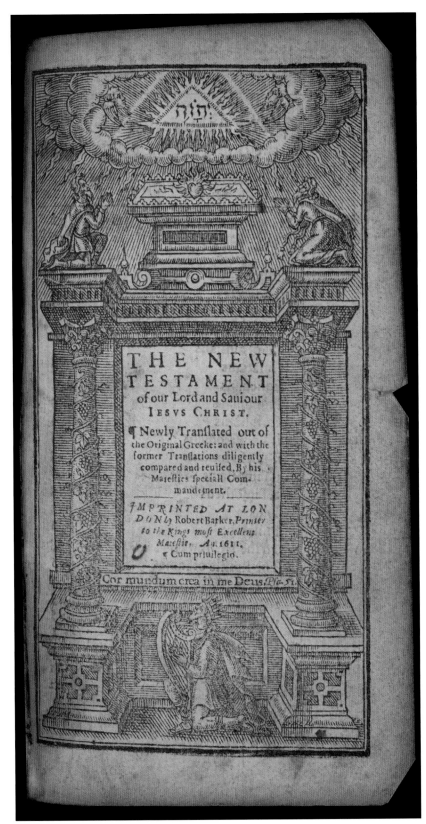

1613, 1611 SHE King James Version

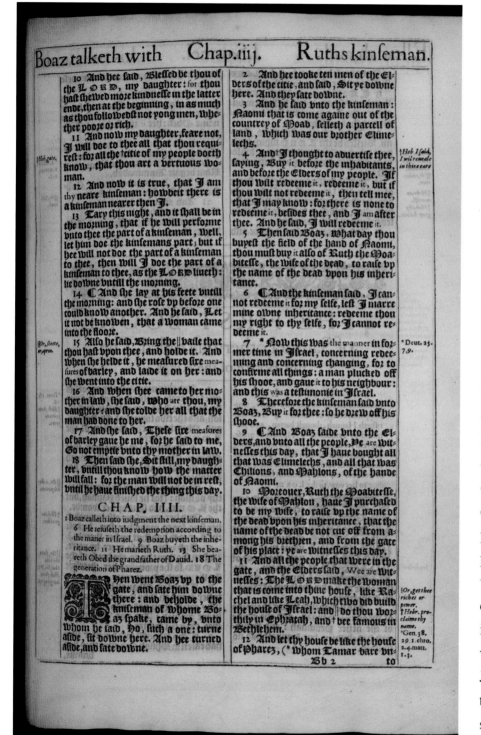

This edition is a hybrid. The New Testament and likely much more of the Bible was published in 1611, as indicated by the New Testament title page. Apparently a fire or flood destroyed portions of the Old Testament published at that time, necessitating the publication of replacement pages in 1613, which introduced one noteworthy divergence from the original translation. This is called the Great SHE Bible because it is not a true first edition of the King James Bible, as evident in the text of Ruth 3:15. The Bible is opened to the passage in question. The first edition printing rendered the phrase in question "*he* went into the citie." This edition printed "*she* went into the citie." (Ancient versions vary.) While King James explicitly forbade the use of notes, clearly scriptural cross-references and short descriptive notes were both permissible and necessary.

King James Psalms

King James I was personally invested in biblical translation. This metrical translation of the Psalms appeared after his death. It is a fascinating work that enjoyed great popularity. Metrical translation facilitated the singing of the Psalms in church and aided in memorizing them. The work merged the inspired reign of David with James and the Stuart Dynasty. The book is open to the engraved title page, which provides an interesting contrast to the title page of the first edition HE Bible. The Tetragrammaton (יהוה) is in the center top of the page as if in heaven. Two angels hold in their teeth a banner that flutters in the sky reading "Glory to God in the Highest on earth peace to all men," seemingly a messianic claim about the realm of King James I. The hand of God pierces through the clouds and supports a codex reading The Psalmes of King David. On the bottom left, David, gazing into heaven and suited in armor with his harp at his side, helps support the book. On the right, King James I, dressed in his regalia, his scepter slung over his shoulder, effortlessly supports his side and ironically gazes directly into the face of the reader. It is possible that this might be seen as the hand of God giving the Psalms to David (a common motif in medieval manuscript art) and

also to the divinely appointed Jacobean David (or so he thought), King James I. The larger portion of the general title reads in a much larger font "Translated by King James."

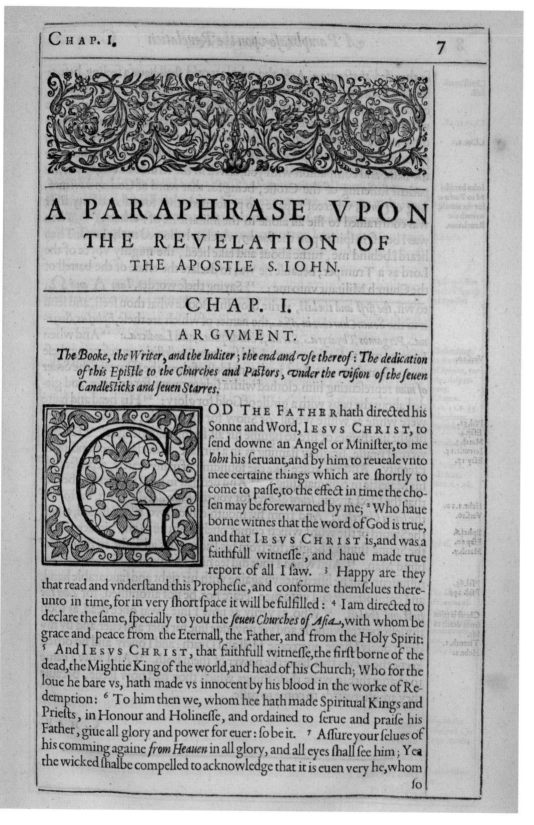

A PARAPHRASE VPON
THE REVELATION OF
THE APOSTLE S. IOHN.

CHAP. I.

ARGVMENT.

The Booke, the Writer, and the Inditer; the end and vse thereof: The dedication of this Epistle to the Churches and Pastors, vnder the vision of the seuen Candlesticks and seuen Starres.

OD THE FATHER hath directed his Sonne and Word, IESVS CHRIST, to send downe an Angel or Minister, to me *Iohn* his seruant, and by him to reueale vnto mee certaine things which are shortly to come to passe, to the effect in time the chosen may be forewarned by me; ² Who haue borne witnes that the word of God is true, and that IESVS CHRIST is, and was a faithfull witnesse, and haue made true report of all I saw. ³ Happy are they that read and vnderstand this Prophesie, and conforme themselues thereunto in time, for in very short space it will be fulfilled: ⁴ I am directed to declare the same, specially to you the *seuen Churches of Asia*, with whom be grace and peace from the Eternall, the Father, and from the Holy Spirit: ⁵ And IESVS CHRIST, that faithfull witnesse, the first borne of the dead, the Mightie King of the world, and head of his Church; Who for the loue he bare vs, hath made vs innocent by his blood in the worke of Redemption: ⁶ To him then we, whom hee hath made Spiritual Kings and Priests, in Honour and Holinesse, and ordained to serue and praise his Father, giue all glory and power for euer: so be it. ⁷ Assure your selues of his comming againe *from Heauen* in all glory, and all eyes shall see him; Yea the wicked shalbe compelled to acknowledge that it is euen very he, whom

so

King James I, Workes, 1616—Paraphrase of Revelation.

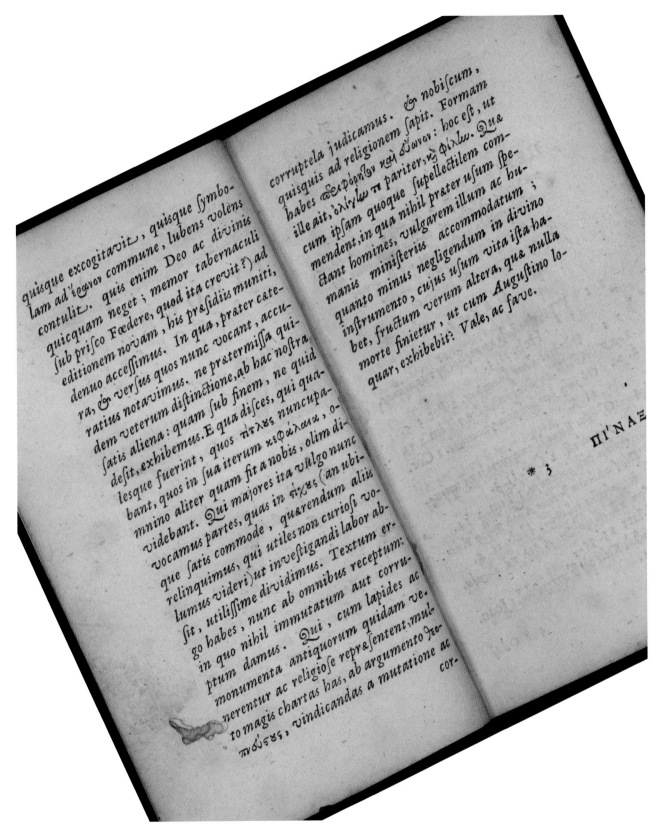

Elziver Greek New Testament, 1633.

Portrait of King James I.

Vera Effigies Reuerendi in Christo
Patris Dñi: Lancecloti Andrewes
Epiſcopi Wintonienſis,

BIOGRAPHY: Lancelot Andrewes (d. 1626) was an English clergyman and scholar who held high positions in the Church of England during the reigns of Queen Elizabeth I and King James I. Andrewes served successively as bishop of Chichester, Ely, and Winchester and oversaw the translation of the King James Bible. Andrewes was educated at Cambridge and at Oxford. He enjoyed an active preaching and academic career. Upon the accession of James I, he rose into great favor because of his methodical style of preaching. He assisted at James's coronation, and in 1604 took part in the Hampton Court Translation Conference. Andrewes's name is first on the list appointed to translate the King James Bible. He directed the First Westminster Company, which was responsible for the translation of Genesis through 2 Kings. He was also the general editor over the entire project.

As a churchman, he was a High Church Anglican, equally removed from the Puritans and the Catholics. Andrewes preached regularly before King James I. The sermons were used to promulgate the doctrine of the Divine Right of Kings. His best-known work is the *Manual of Private Devotions*, which was extremely popular. Andrewes's other works fill eight volumes. Ninety-six of his sermons were published in 1631 by command of King Charles I. He was considered the most highly educated minister in his day, besides Bishop Ussher, and enjoyed an outstanding reputation as an eloquent and impassioned preacher.

CHAPTER TWELVE

The Royal Print Shop

The Royal Print Shop Exhibit Gallery

TIMELINE: The books associated with the Royal Print Shop include the Wife Beater's Bible, 1537, through the final revision of the King James Bible in 1768.

GEOGRAPHICAL RANGE: The items on display in the Royal Print Shop were published in the Netherlands, Germany, and England.

THE SETTING: This room is a re-creation of the Royal Print Shop of Robert Barker. In the center of the room is an exact reproduction of the printing press used to print the first edition of the King James Bible in 1611. No doubt a number of presses would have been busy producing the King James Bible. Robert Barker was not known as the best businessman. What promised to be a lucrative business, because of the license from the king to print the King James Bible, was squandered by Barker. He is woefully understaffed for the work assigned him. Consequently his staff will certainly seek help from bystanders. If you are asked to help, by all means, roll up your sleeves and help Robert Baker's people get their work done.

The room is filled with cases showing examples of typographical errors made by the compositors. Each letter with all of the unusual shapes and signs had to be laid out by the compositor upside down and in reverse order. This used to be the work of scholars, but printers like Barker began hiring young apprentices for cheaper labor. Unfortunately they did not always deliver the best results, though the Bible required the best. As you will see, typographical errors did not begin with Barker and the King James Bible. There are also examples of famous Bibles with odd renderings and sometimes offensive notes, especially to women. There is also a case that contains carefully printed editions of the King James Bible culminating with the 1768 edition, which provided the basic standard text for the present-day King James Bible.

A table has been laid out with tests to see how well one proofreads the biblical text! Take your time and be careful. You will see that problems with textual transmission did not come to an end with the printing age. Printing presented a new set of challenges that required great caution. Mistakes in a manuscript seemed minor when compared to mistakes mass produced on the printing press. Robert Barker would be the first to tell you that the stakes were high! See how many mistakes you can find. If you do an exemplar (a small play on words) job, you may obtain a job in the Barker Print Shop. Good luck.

I knew a time when great care was given to printing the Bible, especially
meticulous compositors and the very best correctors were employed.
The workers were mature and highly educated men, sober about their faith.
Even the paper and font that they used was of the very highest quality.
But now, alas, the best paper is always out-of-stock.
Compositors are mere boys, cheap to hire.
And the correctors are illiterate.

- George Abbot, archbishop of Canterbury (d. 1633) (Revised)

A common laborer in Robert Barker's print shop complains of endless work and meager pay.

Geneva Bible, also known as the Breeches Bible.

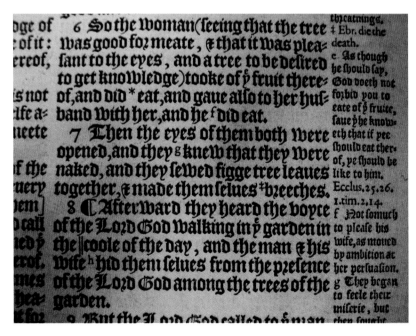

Wife-Beaters Bible, 1537

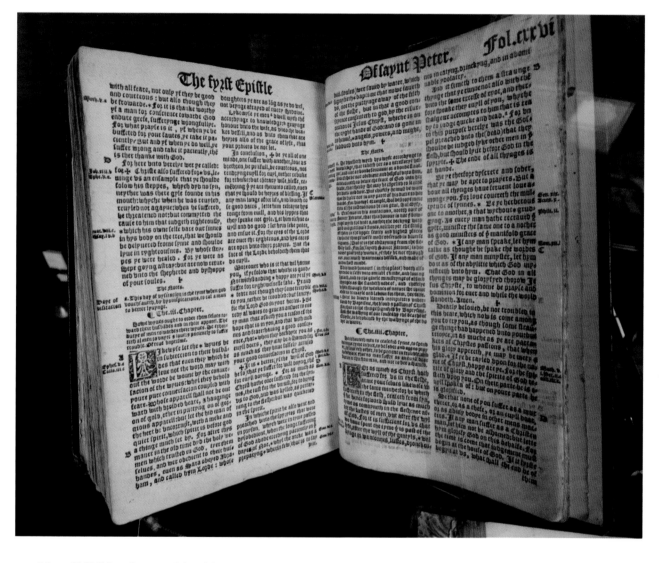

Not all Bibles featured in this room have typographical errors. Some have unfortunate renderings. One of the best-known examples of the latter is the so-called Wife-Beater's Bible. It is actually the Matthew's Bible that first appeared in 1537. This Bible was the work of John Rogers, whose pen name was Thomas Matthew. He combined extensive portions of the Old Testament translated by William Tyndale with the translation found in Coverdale's Old Testament printed in 1535. The New Testament was a reprint of Tyndale's New Testament.

Rogers also added about 2,000 notes, many of them controversial. The marginal note at 1 Peter 3:7 says, in part, "If [the wife] be not obedient and healpfull unto [her husband, he] endeavoureth to beate the feare of God into her." The version was quickly dubbed the Wife-Beater's Bible, indicating that the stray note was considered inappropriate early-on, attracting both ridicule and harsh criticism.

Kilburne's Dangerous Errors in Several Late Printed Bibles, 1659

This little tract raises a concern about sloppy printing errors in Bibles, the potential dangers posed by them to people of faith, and ways to remedy the problems. It also lists some of the many errors found predominately in King James Bibles printed between 1611 and the 1650s. Misprints with Bibles did not begin with the advent of the King James Bible and the mass production of that version for the general public. There are classic examples in some earlier versions, as well.

The short tract is open to the title page. The subtitle is telling: "To the great scandal, and corruption of sound and true Religion." The erudition of the author, William Kilburne, who refers to himself merely as a Gentleman, is shown in his choice of Latin quotations at the bottom of the page. They translate: "Large fires start with small sparks" (an unattributed Latin proverb) and "Resist beginnings; the prescription comes too late when the disease has gained strength after long delay" (Ovid, *Remedia Amoris*, 91).

Wicked Bible, 1631

This Bible has one of the most notorious typographical errors in history. This is an octavo edition of the King James Bible printed in 1631 by the royal printer Robert Barker, containing one of the best-known typographical errors in printing history. The seventh commandment, as recorded in Exodus 20:14, famously omits the word "not," rendering the passage, "Thou shalt commit adultery." When the error was spotted, it was immediately corrected. Some 1,000 copies were destroyed and the printer was heavily fined for his carelessness. Nevertheless, a few copies remained in circulation, making this copy extremely rare.

There has been undue speculation as to whether this was an intentional error or a juvenile prank by a compositor or even an act of vengeance. But the fact that a corrected copy was produced by the printers and bound in the original binding clearly indicates that once the error was discovered, they immediately corrected it and continued with the printing. The corrected copy is also extremely rare. The consequences forced Robert Barker into bankruptcy. The once rich and famous Royal Printer, from an illustrious tradition of printers, died in shame in debtors' prison unable to recover from the loss.

King James Version, 1768

The publication of the first edition of the King James Bible was one that was fraught with errors. Many of these were corrected over time, and others were not. Several concerted efforts were made to correct the text of the King James Bible that culminated with the publication of the 1768 King James Bible, representing a corrected text. Subsequent King James Version Bibles followed the text of this 1768 edition.

The parable of the vinegar.

S. Luke.

The Sadducees convinced.

chief priests and the scribes came upon him, with the elders,

2 And spake unto him, saying, Tell us, By what authority doest thou these things? or who is he that gave thee this authority?

3 And he answered and said unto them, I will also ask you one thing; and answer me.

4 The Baptism of John, was it from heaven, or of men?

5 And they reasoned with themselves, saying, If we shall say, From heaven; he will say, Why then believed ye him not?

6 But and if we say, Of men; all the people will stone us: for they be perswaded that John was a prophet.

7 And they answered, that they could not tell whence it was.

8 And Jesus said unto them, Neither tell I you by what authority I do these things.

9 Then began he to speak to the people this parable; ᵇ A certain man planted a vineyard, and let it forth to husbandmen, and went into a far country for a long time.

10 And at the season, he sent a servant to the husbandmen, that they should give him of the fruit of the vineyard: but the husbandmen beat him, and sent him away empty.

11 And again he sent another servant; and they beat him also, and entreated him

scribes the same hour sought to lay hands on him; and they feared the people: for they perceived that he had spoken this parable against them.

20 And they watched him, and sent forth spies, which should feign themselves just men, that they might take hold of his words, that so they might deliver him unto the power and authority of the governour.

21 And they asked him, saying, ᵈ Master, we know that thou sayest and teachest rightly, neither acceptest thou the person of any, but teachest the way of God ∥ truly.

22 Is it lawful for us to give tribute unto Cesar, or no?

23 But he perceived their craftiness, and said unto them, Why tempt ye me?

24 Shew me a ∥ peny: whose image and superscription hath it? They answered and said, Cesars.

25 And he said unto them, Render therefore unto Cesar the things which be Cesars, and unto God the things which be Gods.

26 And they could not take hold of his words before the people: and they marvelled at his answer, and held their peace.

27 ¶ ᵉ Then came to him certain of the Sadducees (which deny that there is

*King James Bible,
also known as the
Cannibals Bible, 1682.*

*King James Bible,
also known as the
Vinegar Bible, 1717.*

BIOGRAPHY: Robert Barker (d. 1645) was a printer to King James I of England. He was son of Christopher Barker, famous printer for Queen Elizabeth I. Robert Barker's most notable achievement was the printing of the King James Bible, the most influential and important book ever printed in English. He began working with his father in 1589 and inherited the business ten years later. Most of his work was official in nature but also included Bibles, the *Book of Common Prayer,* and legal tomes. He printed the first edition of the King James Bible in 1611. Despite the fact that the translation was sponsored by King James I, Barker financed the printing. He earned little from it but prestige. It was not considered an elegant printing. It had uneven lines. He used old-fashioned black-letter font, and it contained a number of mistakes that needed to be corrected.

In 1631 Robert Barker and Martin Lucas, both royal printers in London, published a Bible with a notorious typographical error. In the printing of Exodus 20:14 the word *not* was omitted in the sentence "Thou shalt not commit adultery." The mistake was caught and immediately corrected. Only 11 uncorrected copies are known to survive. King Charles I and the archbishop were outraged. The printers were fined £300 (nearly $100,000 today) and were stripped of their printers' licenses. Barker was imprisoned for the mistake in 1635. He spent his last decade in and out of prison and lost his business along with his family's esteemed reputation.

CHAPTER THIRTEEN

THE ARTISTS' STUDIO

The Artists' Studio Exhibit Gallery

TIMELINE: The beautifully illustrated books associated with the Artists' Studio range in date from a tenth-century Greek Psalter written in gold to prints by Salvador Dali illustrating sequences from the life of Moses dating to 1978.

GEOGRAPHICAL RANGE: The items on display in the Artists' Studio originated in Greece, Turkey, France, Spain, Austria, Germany, Italy, Israel, England, and the United States.

THE SETTING: The Artists' Studio is filled with Bibles richly illustrated and beautifully adorned from the cover to the painted edges of the page. A live artist works busily in the corner illustrating a biblical theme. Visitors are greeted by an animated engraving by one of the most illustrious modern Bible illustrators, Paul Gustave Doré (d. 1883). The scene might not look familiar to some or may be confused with other Bible stories. It is a picture from the Old Testament apocryphal work called Judith, which has inspired artists (as it has readers) throughout the ages. The book tells how a beautiful Jewish widow risked her reputation, pretending to take an interest in a Babylonian general who was encamped with his troops surrounding Jerusalem. She went into his tent and killed him. The heroic woman emerged from the tent, silencing the murmurings, holding the general's severed head by his hair. But Doré's engraving is animated. The general tells the story of his fate at Judith's hands and continues to tell the story of the artist who left him in this embarrassing and shameful predicament—Paul Gustave Doré.

Throughout history art has been used to help with the interpretation of a text, as with line drawings, illuminated manuscripts, woodcuts, and engravings. Works by some of the most illustrious artists are on display. A number of works were commissioned by kings and emperors. A variety of regional styles are also depicted. The use of gold and silver had enormous symbolic importance to illustrate the purity of the word and also as a medium to reflect light across the page, allowing it to be read with greater ease by candlelight. One case contains a wide variety of fore-edged paintings (a technique where painting is done on outer or fore edges of a book's pages and is revealed only when the pages are layered back) by some of the most famous artists employing this medium. Some paintings illustrate biblical scenes, while others are landscapes or even quaint reminiscences of country life. Several cases are filled with all sorts of interesting bindings.

The Artists' Studio underscores the enormously important role that art has had with the production of the Bible throughout time. A table is set up for any promising artists to hand-color their own woodcuts. Take your time in this room. For centuries, art was incorporated into the Bible; it was an expected feature. But now it is no longer customary for the reader; perhaps it's even a distraction. In the modern world, the Bible is typically black and white, and the only pictures are an occasional map. How and why do these changes in perception and design come about? Take some time to reflect on these trends as you encounter some great attempts to illuminate and adorn the Bible and enhance the readers' experience.

The biblical text has been a canvas
more frequently used by more artists
across more media than any other work ever written.
To know the Bible is to know art.
And to know biblical art is to know the soul of the artist.

\- Anonymous

An artist welcomes visitors to his shop
and invites them to enjoy the beautifully
illustrated Bibles on display.

Ethiopian Miracles of Mary with other Marian Texts, 18th Century

The Ethiopian Church has the most expansive canon of all Christian traditions. The Ethiopians were converted to Christianity during the reign of Ezana II about the time of the Emperor Constantine. Africa has a Christian legacy that is older than the conversion of the Roman Empire. Ethiopic manuscripts contain rich apocryphal traditions about Mary and the saints, and their texts, like this fascinating one, are richly illustrated with exotic African art depicting the biblical world. The manuscript shows the three Magi dressed in magnificent robes. They have come to pay homage to the infant King. Two kneel in reverence, and the third gazes in wonder over their shoulders. They are aligned as if to show a depth of field. The star hovers above the Holy Family's abode, and a ray of light shines down on the baby Jesus. The Magi are depicted as kings themselves, and two set aside their crowns in adoration of the King of Kings. The baby Jesus reaches out—innocent, a bit timid. The Virgin Mary gently holds the child and looks in wonder at the scene. On the top right, an angel in a cloud brandishing a sword warns the Magi not to return to King Herod the Great.

Psalter, Master of Jaques de Besançon, Paris circa 1480–1490

This manuscript is of enormous importance because it is almost identical to one that was illustrated very likely by the same artist for the French king Charles VIII. It contains the Psalms, Calendar, Canticles, and liturgical materials for corporate worship and private devotion, enhanced by one of the most accomplished Parisian artists of the day. The miniatures do not merely illustrate the page; they are objects of meditation and enhance the written folio and provide a venue for a deeper, personal response by the reader. The manuscript is open to a full-page illumination for Psalm 68. The illumination shows King David standing unclothed in the Jordan River. Apparently he is only wearing his crown. He stands motionless in the flowing water, towering above the local landscape, praying to God. David's forehead is slightly wrinkled, and his bare body is drawn by the artist with

meticulous precision. David stands bare and vulnerable before his Lord in penance and devotion. The anatomic accuracy of the artist's depiction of David's body would indicate that the artist had studied models from the Italian Renaissance. The landscape includes deep vistas with fanciful buildings in the far distance. The connection between King David and his Lord was an intentional motif that reinforced the connection between the French royalty and God. This representation is particularly poignant with respect to Psalm 68, which exalts the sovereignty of God, His rule over the earth, His bountiful mercies, and His invincible power. King David, the anointed ruler over Israel and powerful warlord, stands naked in abject submission, empty and needy before all that God is and has done.

Mysteria Passionis Domini Nostri Iesu Christi, Georg Scherer and Illustrated after Albrecht Dürer, 1591

This fascinating book contains a copy of one the most celebrated sets of engravings on the Passion of Christ by Albrecht Dürer with a manuscript of meditational prayers on the Mystery of the Passion by an illustrious Jesuit preacher named Georg Scherer. The work was commissioned by a Jesuit for one of his pupils, the Archduke Ferdinand of Austria and future Kaiser Ferdinand II. The manuscript is open to an engraving of the Agony in the Garden. While the disciples sleep, Jesus Christ, in His last earthly hours, prays to His Father in heaven. His hands are raised. An angel surrounded by the radiant glory of heaven descends in a cloud, his wings furling. He extends a cross. In Matthew 26:39 the Gospel text says that when Jesus prayed in the Garden, He "fell on his face, and prayed, saying, O my Father, if it be possible, let this cup pass from me: nevertheless not as I will, but as thou wilt" (KJV). The cup is typically associated with the transference of the sin of the world to Jesus as the Lamb of God, indicating His concern was with the separation that would take place between Himself and the Father. In the engraving it appears that Jesus has reconciled Himself to the Father's will and has risen up to embrace the destiny of the cross.

Calligraphic Psalter in German, 1592

This is a magnificent masterpiece of calligraphy and micrography in its original binding composed for Count John VII of Oldenburg. The manuscript contains Luther's translation of the Psalms. The artistry and calligraphic style show the influence of Jewish calligraphic techniques. It is well known that Jewish and Christian scribes and artists worked together very closely, enhancing each other's divine work. The manuscript is open to a micrographic design in mirror writing around the Ten Commandments. It is part of the introductory material preceding the Psalms and shows the masterful skills of Johannes Kirchring the Elder, one of the greatest 17th-century calligraphers. This page is especially noteworthy. The calligrapher uses gold and silver metallic ink here and

throughout the manuscript, vividly illustrating the purity of the Scriptures, affirmed in the Psalms themselves. The center of this page features the Ten Commandments on tablets. The surrounding writing is in mirror, which is formed by writing in the direction that is the reverse of the ordinary way for a given language. The artistic style of writing shows the direct influence of Jewish calligraphers and an appreciation for their strict yet exquisite approach to illustrating the Scripture. This volume exemplifies the close ties that existed between Jews and Christians involved in the common task of copying the Scriptures.

Fore-edged painting of the Last Supper.

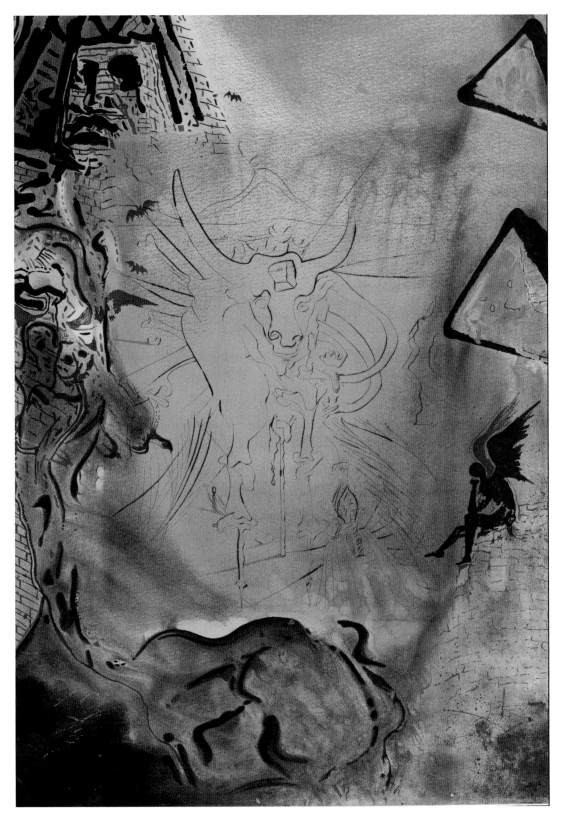

Salvador Dali Print: **The Dream of Moses.**

*Paul Gustave Doré,
engraving of Judith.*

BIOGRAPHY: Paul Gustave Doré (d. 1883) was a French artist, engraver, illustrator, and sculptor. Doré worked primarily in wood and steel engraving. He was born in Strasbourg, and he published his first illustrated story at the age of 15. As a young man, he won commissions to illustrate scenes from books by Rabelais, Balzac, Milton, and Dante. Doré was asked to illustrate the works of Lord Byron and later the Bible. He also illustrated a French edition of Cervantes's *Don Quixote* and an oversized edition of Poe's "The Raven" the year of his death at a relatively young age after a short illness.

Doré's illustrations of the Bible were an enormous success and were reprinted with text of many languages. The publication of the illustrated Bible in English led to an exhibition of his work in London and ultimately to the opening of the Doré Gallery in London. The engravings illustrated the great dramatic events in Scripture with mystery, pathos, and vivid imagination. The individual engravings are highly collectible, and many of the images are iconographic. His success with the Bible led to a project to create 180 engravings illustrating the city of London. While a financial success, some critics accused Doré of focusing on poverty in parts of London. Doré was primarily celebrated in his day for his paintings, which were world-renowned, but he is best remembered for his woodcuts and engravings. And his most beloved and popular illustrations were those of the Bible.

CHAPTER FOURTEEN

THE TENT OF DISCOVERY

The Tent of Discovery Exhibit Gallery

TIMELINE: The items in the Tent of Discovery range in date from the two silver amulets, discovered in a late seventh-century BCE grave, to Codex Sinaiticus, which dates to the mid-fourth century CE.

GEOGRAPHICAL RANGE: The items in the Tent of Discovery come from Israel and Egypt.

THE SETTING: The setting resembles an archaeological tent filled with the significant discoveries of manuscripts that have a bearing on the text and transmission of the Bible since the first appearance of the King James Bible. Numerous important discoveries have been made, particularly since the 19th century. This coincides with the emergence of archaeology as a new scientific inquiry, the colonial exploitation of countries such as Egypt, and a new market created for individuals and institutions that had interests in collecting biblical antiquities. This had an impact on biblical translation, providing earlier and often superior texts of the Bible. In addition, scholars were able to attain a more precise understanding of biblical languages, bringing greater clarity to the meaning of the text. Archaeological discoveries of biblical cities, historical and cultural records, and the material of the biblical world have provided important background information that has clarified the meaning of the biblical text. Another important development has been the growth of linguistic theory, which has helped translators with a more scientific approach, resulting in a more understandable and meaningful translation.

It should be noted that although the King James Bible was a landmark in Bible translation, the Old Testament text was essentially based on a single manuscript dating to around 1100 CE. Today more than 35,000 manuscripts of the Old Testament survive in a number of ancient languages of varying textual importance. Fragments of Hebrew texts have been discovered dating slightly earlier than the text used by the King James translators. Complete texts of the Greek translation of the Old Testament, of enormous significance, date to the fourth and fifth centuries CE, and fragments date much earlier. Hebrew, Aramaic, and some Greek manuscripts dating between 250 BCE and 135 CE were discovered in the Judean Desert (commonly called the Dead Sea Scrolls) between the late 1940s and the early 1960s. The biblical manuscripts provided texts that dated between 1,000 and 1,250 years earlier than any previously known Hebrew or Aramaic biblical texts. They illustrate the complexity of the versions that were in circulation and the great care that *sofers* (or *soferim*) took to copy the text accurately.

With regard to the New Testament, a handful of Greek manuscripts were used by the translators that formed the text. None were earlier than the tenth century CE. Currently more than 5,700 Greek manuscripts survive, a number from the second century, including complete Gospels dating to around the end of the second century. The earliest complete Greek New Testament dates to around 350 CE. When all ancient languages are taken into consideration, there are some 25,000 manuscripts of the New Testament, vastly expanding our understanding of the biblical text. Considering that many of the texts numbered for the Old Testament come from the same manuscripts as those numbered for the New Testament, the total number of biblical manuscripts in ancient languages appears to be in excess of 40,000.

A docent interacting with visitors—bringing the *Passages* experience to life.

As a result, calls were made for new translations. Charges were made that people wanted to tamper with the Bible. In 1881 a revision of the King James Bible appeared, with no little controversy. Although alternate translations existed prior to this time, this opened the door for the dissemination of new translations of Scripture. Despite this, the King James, through William Tyndale's translations, continued to affect the language of the text and the overall religious psyche. Furthermore, the King James continued to be the most-sold translation through the 20th century.

This Tent of Discovery celebrates some of the more important biblical discoveries.

Ancient Biblical papyri offer the most important discoveries since Codex Sinaiticus.
The biblical manuscripts date so close to their original compositions
that their authenticity is without debate.
No other ancient text has such early and abundant evidence of its text.
No unbiased scholar would deny that the biblical text survived substantially sound.
- Sir Frederic Kenyon, former keeper of manuscripts at the British Library (Revised)

Codex Sinaiticus

The celebrated Codex Sinaiticus was discovered in the mid-19th century by the minister, scholar, and text-critic Constantine von Tischendorf at the Monastery of Mt. St. Catherine's on the Sinai Peninsula at the foot of Jebel Musa or the traditional site of Mt. Sinai. Tischendorf painstakingly gathered the disparate leaves over the course of several decades and negotiated their eventual acquisition. The Greek uncial manuscript dated to the mid-fourth century and contained most of the Old Testament and the entire New Testament with additional materials.

The manuscript provided a Greek text to the Old Testament produced more than 600 years earlier than any previously discovered manuscript, albeit in Greek not Hebrew. The New Testament portion of the manuscript was earlier than any previously known manuscript and revealed the earliest-known text of the New Testament to date. Despite the subsequent discovery of numerous papyri of the New Testament that date earlier than the Codex Sinaiticus, its importance in the reconstruction of the text of the New Testament cannot be overestimated. Tischendorf's discovery opened the door to a new approach to the study of the text of the Greek New Testament which had been dominated by manuscripts dating more than six centuries later.

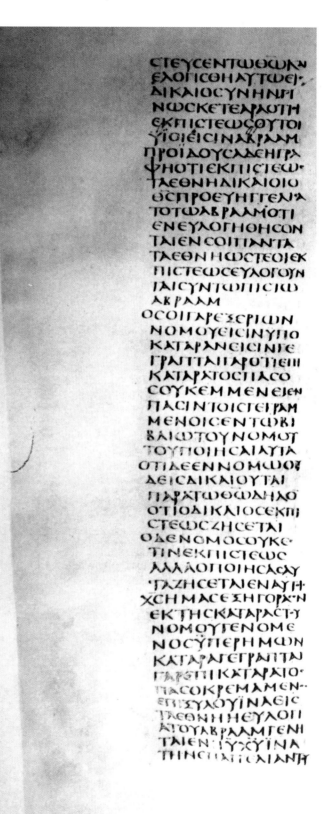

ΠΝ CΛ ΔΒΩΜΕΝ Ν
ΑΤΗ CΠΙCΤΕΩC Α
ΔΕΛΦΟΙ ΚΑΤΑ ΑΝ
ΘΡΩΠΟΝ ΛΕΓΩ Ο
ΜΩ C ΑΝΘΡΩΠΟΥ
ΚΕΚΥΡΩΜΕΝΗΝ
ΔΙΑΘΗΚΗΝ ΟΥΔΙ·
ΑΘΕΤΕΙ Η ΕΠΙΔΙΑΤ·
CΕΤΑΙ ΤΩ ΔΕ ΑΒΡΑΑΜ
ΕΡΡΕΘΗCΑΝ ΑΙ ΕΠΑΝ
ΓΕΛΙΑΙ ΚΑΙ ΤΩ CΠ
ΜΑΤΙ ΑΥΤΟΥ ΟΥΛΕ
ΚΑΙ ΤΟΙ C CΠΕΡΜΑ
ΩC ΕΠΙ ΠΟΛΛΩΝ
ΑΛΛΩ C ΕΦ ΕΝΟ C
ΚΑΙ ΤΩ CΠΕΡΜΑΤΙ
COΥ ΟC ΕCΤΙΝ XC
ΤΟΥΤΟ ΔΕ ΛΕΓΩ ΔΙ
ΑΘΗΚΗΝ ΠΡΟ ΚΕ
ΚΥΡΩΜΕΝΗΝ ΥΠ
ΤΟΥ ΘΥ Ο ΜΕΤΑ ΤΕ
ΤΡΑΚΟCΙΑ ΚΑΙ ΤΡΙΑ
ΚΟΝΤΑ ΕΤΗ ΓΕΓΟ
ΝΩC ΝΟΜΟC ΟΥ
ΚΑΚΥΡΟΙ ΕΙC ΤΟ ΚΑ
ΤΑΡΓΗCΑΙ ΤΗΝ ΕΠ
ΓΕΛΙΑΝ ΕΙ ΓΑΡ ΕΚ
ΝΟΜΟΥ Η ΚΛΗΡΟ
ΝΟΜΙΑ ΟΥΚΕΤΙ Ε
Ξ ΕΠΑΓΓΕΛΙΑC ΤΩ
ΔΕ ΑΒΡΑΑΜ ΔΙ ΕΠΑΝ
ΓΕΛΙΑC ΚΕΧΑΡΙCΤΑΙ
Ο ΘC
ΤΙ ΟΥΝ Ο ΝΟΜΟC Ω
ΠΑΡΑΒΑCΕΩΝ ΧΑ
ΡΙΝ ΠΡΟCΕΤΕΘΗ ΑΧ
ΡΙ C ΟΥ ΕΛΘΗ ΤΟ CΠ
ΜΑ Ω ΕΠΗΓΓΕΛΤΑΙ
ΔΙΑΤΑΓΕΙ C ΔΙ ΑΓΓΕ
ΛΩΝ ΕΝ ΧΙΡΙ ΜΕCΙ
ΤΟΥ Ο ΔΕ ΜΕCΙΤΗC·
ΝΟC ΟΥΚ ΕCΤΙΝ Ο
ΔΕ ΘC ΕΙC ΕCΤΙΝ
Ο ΟΥΝ ΝΟΜΟC ΚΑ
ΤΑ ΤΩΝ ΕΠΑΓΓΕΛΙ
ΩΝ ΤΟΥ ΘΥ ΜΗ·
ΝΟΙΤΟ ΕΙ ΓΑΡ ΕΔΟ
ΘΗ ΝΟΜΟC Ο ΔΥΝΑ

ΜΕΝΟC ΖΩΟΠΟΙΗ
CΑΙ ΟΝΤΩC ΕΚ ΝΟ
ΜΟΥ ΗΝ ΑΝ Η ΔΙΚΑΙ
ΟCΥΝΗ ΑΛΛΑ CΥΝΕ
ΚΑΙCΕΝ Η ΓΡΑΦΗ
ΤΑ ΠΑΝΤΑ ΥΠΟ ΑΜΑΡ
ΤΙΑΝ ΙΝΑ Η ΕΠΑΓΓ
ΛΙΑ ΕΚ ΠΙCΤΕΩC ΙΥ
ΧΥ ΔΟΘΗ ΤΟΙC ΠΙCΤ
ΟΥCΙΝ
ΠΡΟ ΤΟΥ ΔΕ ΕΛΘΙΝ ΤΗ
ΠΙCΤΙΝ ΥΠΟ ΝΟΜ
ΕΦΡΟΥΡΟΥΜΕΘΑ Υ
ΚΑΙΟΜΕΝΟΙ ΕΙC ΤΗ
ΜΕΛΛΟΥCΑΝ ΠΙCΤΙ
ΑΠΟΚΑΛΥΦΘΗΝΑΙ
ΩCΤΕ Ο ΝΟΜΟC ΠΑΙ
ΔΑΓΩΓΟC ΗΜΩΝ
ΓΟΝΕΝ ΕΙC ΧΝ ΙΝΑ
ΕΚ ΠΙCΤΕΩC ΔΙΚΑΙ
ΩΘΩΜΕΝ ΕΛΘΟΥ
CΗC ΔΕ ΤΗC ΠΙCΤΕ
ΩC ΟΥΚΕΤΙ ΥΠΟ ΠΑΙ
ΔΑΓΩΓΟΝ ΕCΜΕΝ
ΠΑΝΤΕC ΓΑΡ ΥΙΟΙ ΘΥ
ΕCΤΕ ΔΙΑ ΤΗC ΠΙCΤ·
ΩC ΕΝ ΧΩ ΙΥ
ΟCΟΙ ΓΑΡ ΕΙC ΧΝ ΕΒΑ
ΠΤΙCΘΗΤΕ ΧΝ ΕΝΕ
CΑCΘΕ ΟΥΚ ΕΝΙ ΙΟΥ
ΔΑΙΟC ΟΥΔΕ ΕΛΛΗΝ
ΟΥΚ ΕΝΙ ΔΟΥΛΟC
ΟΥΔΕ ΕΛΕΥΘΕΡΟC ΟΥ
ΚΕΝΙ ΑΡCΕΝ ΚΑΙ ΘΗ
ΛΥ ΠΑΝΤΕC ΓΑΡ ΥΜ
ΕΙC ΕΙC ΕCΤΕ ΕΝ ΧΩ ΙΥ
ΕΙ ΔΕ ΥΜΕΙC ΧΥ ΑΡΑ
ΤΟΥ ΑΒΡΑΑΜ CΠΕΡ
ΜΑ ΕCΤΕ ΚΑΤ ΕΠΑΓΓ
ΓΕΛΙΑΝ ΚΛΗΡΟΝΟ
ΛΕΓΩ ΔΕ ΕΦ ΟCΟΝ
ΧΡΟΝΟΝ Ο ΚΛΗΡΟ
ΝΟΜΟC ΝΗΠΙΟC
ΕCΤΙΝ ΟΥΔΕΝ ΔΙΑ
ΦΕΡΕΙ ΔΟΥΛΟΥ ΚC ΠΑ
ΤΩΝ ΩΝ ΑΛΛΑ ΥΠ
ΕΠΙΤΡΟΠΟΥC ΕCΤΙ
ΚΑΙ ΟΙΚΟΝΟΜΟΥ

ΑΧΡΙ ΤΗC ΠΡΟΘΕCΜΙ
ΑC ΤΟΥ ΠΑΤΡΟC
ΟΥΤΩC ΚΑΙ ΗΜΙC ΟΤ
ΗΜΕΝ ΝΗΠΙΟΙ ΥΠ
ΤΑ CΤΟΙΧΙΑ ΤΟΥ ΚΟCΜ
ΗΜΕΘΑ ΔΕΔΟΥΛΩ
ΜΕΝΟΙ ΟΤΕ ΔΕ ΗΛΘ
ΤΟ ΠΛΗΡΩΜΑ ΤΟΥ
ΧΡΟΝΟΥ ΕΞΑΠΕCΤΙ
ΛΕΝ Ο ΘC ΤΟΝ ΥΝ ΑΥ
ΤΟΥ ΓΕΝΟΜΕΝΟΝ ΕΚ
ΓΥΝΑΙΚΟC ΓΕΝΟΜ
ΝΟΝ ΥΠΟ ΝΟΜΟΝ
ΙΝΑ ΤΟΥC ΥΠΟ ΝΟ
ΜΟΝ ΕΞΑΓΟΡΑCΗ
ΝΑ ΤΗΝ ΥΙΟΘΕCΙΑΝ
ΑΠΟΛΑΒΩΜΕΝ
ΟΤΙ ΔΕ ΕCΤΕ ΥΙΟΙ ΕΞΑ
ΠΕCΤΙΛΕΝ Ο ΘC ΤΟ
ΠΝΑ ΤΟΥ ΥΙΟΥ ΑΥΤ·
ΕΙC ΤΑC ΚΑΡΔΙΑC Η
ΜΩΝ ΚΡΑΖΟΝ ΑΒΒΑ
Ο ΠΑΤΗΡ ΩCΤΕ ΟΥΚ
ΕΤΙ ΕΙ ΔΟΥΛΟC ΑΛΛΑ
ΥΙΟC ΕΙ ΔΕ ΥΙΟC ΚΑΙ
ΚΛΗΡΟΝΟΜΟC ΔΙ
Α ΘΥ
ΑΛΛΑ ΤΟΤΕ ΜΕΝ ΟΥ
ΚΕΙ ΔΟΤΕC ΘΝ ΕΔΟΥ
ΛΕΥCΑΤΕ ΤΟΙC ΦΥCΙ
ΜΗ ΟΥCΙ ΘΕΟΙC ΝΥ
ΛΕΓΝΟΝΤΕC ΘΝ
ΜΑΛΛΟΝ ΔΕ ΓΝΩ
CΘΕΝΤΕC ΥΠΟ ΘΥ·
ΠΩC ΕΠΙCΤΡΕΦ
ΤΕ ΠΑΛΙΝ ΕΠΙ ΤΑ Α
CΘΕΝΗ ΚΑΙ ΠΤΩΧΑ
CΤΟΙΧΙΑ ΟΙC ΠΑΛΙ
ΑΝΩΘΕΝ ΔΟΥΛΕΥ
CΕΘΑΙ ΘΕΛΕΤΕ ΗΜΕΡ
ΠΑΡΑΤΗΡΕΙCΘΕ ΚΝ
ΜΗΝΑC ΚΑΙ ΚΑΙ
ΚΑΙ ΕΝΙΑΥΤΟΥC Φ
ΒΟΥΜΑΙ ΥΜΑC ΜΗ
ΠΩC ΕΙΚΗ ΚΕΚΟΠΙ
ΑΚΑ ΕΙC ΥΜΑC
ΓΙΝΕCΘΕ ΩC ΕΓΩ ΟΤΙ
ΚΑΓΩ ΩC ΥΜΙC

The Great Isaiah Scroll, Dead Sea Scrolls

Without debate, the most significant discovery of biblical manuscripts in the 20th century was the discovery of scrolls on the northwest shore of the Dead Sea and later in the surrounding region of the Judean Desert. The initial discoveries were made by Bedouins in 1947, and through systematic excavations at Qumran led by Fr. Roland de Vaux between 1951 and 1956. Texts were discovered in other locations as well through the early 1960s. Tens of thousands of texts were discovered, most small fragments. More than 1,000 texts have been identified, and more than 240 are biblical texts. The only complete biblical scroll contains the entire Book of Isaiah and dates to the mid-third century BCE. The text dates to more than 1,200 years earlier than the oldest known Hebrew manuscript of the entire Old Testament, called the Leningrad Codex. Although different versions of the Old Testament were in circulation at the time the Dead Sea Scrolls were produced, comparing the so-called Great Isaiah Scroll with the text of Isaiah in the Leningrad Codex shows the remarkable care the *sofers* took when copying the text.

Another factor to take into consideration is that the prophet Isaiah lived in the mid-eighth century BCE. This scroll was copied around 500 years later, but from a scroll that probably dated to within 350 years of the original composition, which in itself is remarkable. Furthermore, this is among the earliest of the discovered Dead Sea Scrolls and would have certainly been copied from an important and authoritative scroll taken by the community from Jerusalem. The scroll on exhibit is an exact replica on leather made from the original photographs of the scroll when it was discovered. The original, which is in Israel, has deteriorated significantly. At the museum in Jerusalem dedicated to the Dead Sea Scrolls, called the Shrine of the Book, a similar replica is on display. The discovery of the Dead Sea Scrolls has greatly enhanced our appreciation for the careful work of the *sofer* and the complexity of the textual traditions. They have brought greater clarity to our understanding of the text.

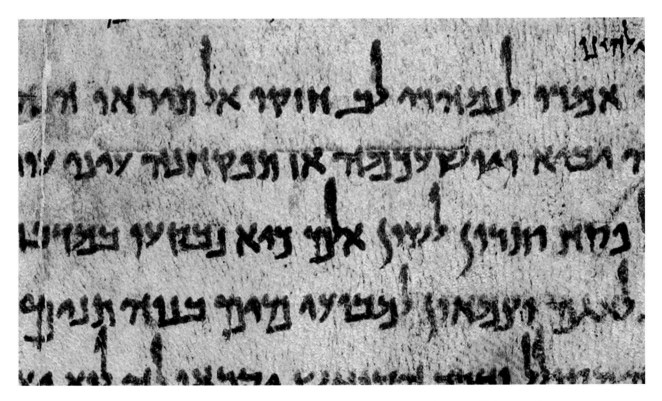

Close-up of a section of text from the Great Isaiah scroll from Qumran.

Papyrus 52 (P52)

The earliest surviving fragment of the New Testament is Papyrus 52, also known as the John Rylands Papyrus, named after the university library where the text resides. The small fragment is from a codex of the Gospel of St. John and contains John 18:31–33 and 37–38. It was discovered in a Roman garbage dump in the Middle Egyptian town of Oxyrhynchus. The site yielded a number of remarkable discoveries of biblical, religious, and classical texts. Excavations were conducted by

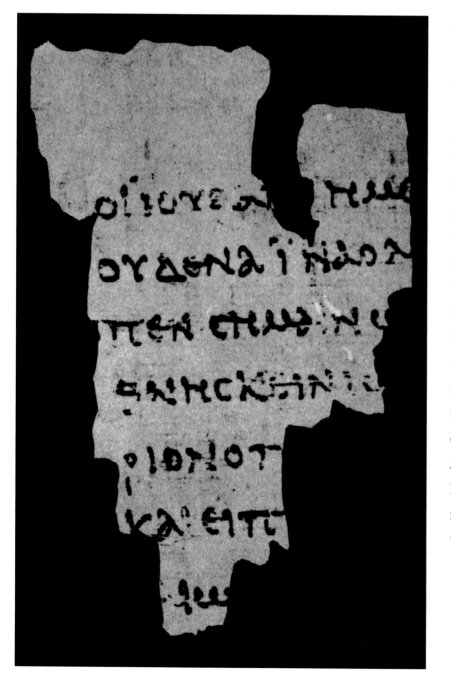

Bernard Grenfell and Arthur Hunt between 1896 and 1906. More than 150,000 papyri are housed at the Sackler Library adjoining the Ashmolean Museum at Oxford University. This particular fragment dates to between 120 and 140 CE, placing its composition within a generation or two of the life of the author. The text was obviously copied from an earlier exemplar. It also illustrates how rapidly Christianity spread. Within a generation of the death of the last apostle, there appears to have been a complete text of the Gospel of John in use in a bustling Roman town in Middle Egypt more than 1,000 miles from where the Gospel was written.

Ketef Hinnom Silver Amulets with the Priestly Benediction

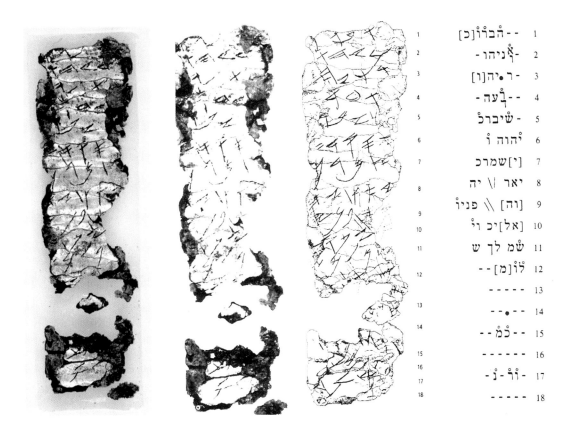

The earliest texts of the Old Testament discovered to date are two thin, silver amulets that contain the Priestly Benediction in Numbers 6:24–26. The texts were rolled and placed in a casing that had disintegrated. They were found in a burial site overlooking the Hinnom Valley by Israeli archaeologist Gabriel Barkay in 1979. Their being found in a burial site helped with the dating of the amulets. The burial dates to around the end of the seventh century BCE or around the time of the Assyrian captivity of Samaria and their failed attempt to capture Jerusalem. Amulets containing prayers and Scripture were commonly worn by Jews and, later, Christians. They were used to ward off evil, to bring God's blessing, and as a reminder of the claims in the verses. Because of the climate in Jerusalem, scrolls of Scripture would not survive as they had in the surrounding desert and along the coast of the Dead Sea. These amulets survived because they were written on silver. Although deteriorated, the surviving text is virtually the same as the modern text. Traditional dates for the life of Moses, the traditionally cited author of Numbers, range between 1450 and 1250 BCE. These amulets indicate that liturgically important texts from Moses' writings were being used as religious jewelry only six to eight centuries after their original composition, which is remarkable.

***Solomon Schechter working on the
Cairo Genizah at Cambridge University.***

Cave 4 at Qumran, site of the discovery of Dead Sea Scrolls.

Monastery of Mt. St. Catherine's, near Mt. Sinai.

BIOGRAPHY: Agnes Smith Lewis (d. 1926) and Margaret Dunlop Gibson (d. 1920) were twin sisters and scholars of Semitic languages—generations ahead of their time in a world dominated by males. Their father was an amateur linguist, and the sisters were fluent in several modern languages and studied a number of ancient languages. Both married in the 1880s but were soon widowed. The twins made several trips to Egypt in search of ancient documents. They were involved in the famous discovery of the Cairo *Genizah* (a closet or storage place where sacred writings were, and still are, retired by Jews). They also went on several expeditions to the Monastery of Mt. St. Catherine's, discovering important Syriac manuscripts and cataloging many others. Over the course of several decades, they also gathered the so-called Codex *Climaci Rescriptus,* which contained early texts of Scripture in Palestinian Aramaic and in Greek.

Although these two extraordinary women were never granted degrees by Cambridge University, which did not admit women until 1948, they received honorary degrees from the universities of Dublin, St. Andrews, Halle, and Heidelberg. The sisters used their inheritance to endow Westminster College in Cambridge, and they gave their private library, which contained the Codex *Climaci Rescriptus* and included the library of the renowned biblical scholar Eberhardt Nestle, to the college. They also helped establish the Presbyterian chaplaincy to the University of Oxford.

CHAPTER FIFTEEN

THE TRANSLATORS' STATION

The Translators' Station Exhibit Gallery

Bible translation is an arduous task, requiring expertise in a variety of ancient languages and the necessary modern languages for scholarly purposes. It also requires an understanding of textual criticism, history, theology, biblical backgrounds, and interpretation, not to mention an astute understanding of the target language of the translation and principles of linguistics. The people of the target language are frequently illiterate, requiring the development of a phonetic system prior to the translation work. The story of Bible translation is, in part, the story of the spread of literacy, which opens a person's soul to the life of the mind and the world of ideas. It also empowers women and is the great equalizer. To view the process of Bible translation as simply a tool for indoctrination would grossly underestimate the currency of literacy—something almost taken for granted in the West.

Some religious traditions, such as Islam, believe that any translation of the original text of their holy book is a distortion. The original writings of the Qur'an do not exist. In fact the author, Muhammad, was himself illiterate and dictated his recitations to his secretary. But the official text of the Qur'an is written in Classical Arabic, which is as far removed from the vast majority of Muslims as the Latin Scriptures were from the masses of medieval Europe.

In contrast to this is Judaism, which has been able to maintain spiritual life and tradition by keeping the reading of the Torah and other Scriptures central to their liturgy. Of course Hebrew is a modern language, as well. Yet for many non-Hebrew–speaking Jews who do not apply themselves to the ritual of reading the Torah in Hebrew (beyond their Bar or Bat Mitzvah), the language and the text can be lost. There was a time after the Babylonian captivity when Hebrew became a dead language, used only in liturgical contexts by the educated or religiously trained—which meant almost exclusively males.

It had been replaced by the language of the Babylonian conquerors—Aramaic. So the Jews returned from captivity reading a translation of the Scriptures called the Targum, which is Hebrew with an interlinear Aramaic translation. The priest Ezra makes reference to the use of a Targum when he consecrated the people returning to Jerusalem by reading the Law. Eventually the Greek translation of the Hebrew Bible became the one most commonly used by most Jews and early Christians. In fact, one might suggest that the value of using a translation that could be understood by many was endorsed by Jesus Himself. He commonly quoted from the Greek Old Testament, presumably to influence the people with His message. Ironically, according to the Greek text of the New Testament, Jesus' erudite opponents in debate with Him often quoted from the Hebrew Bible, which must have fallen on the deaf ears of the crowd, since the vast majority of people couldn't understand Hebrew.

The story of *Passages* has shown the indefatigable efforts of translators over time who had a passion to share the Bible with those who had lost or never had access to it. None of the translators were ever content with their work. They were always correcting it, perfecting it, adapting it to modern expressions, and taking into consideration new textual and linguistic insights. It is a tireless, thankless labor of heartfelt devotion. With every word or every turn of a phrase, the weight of the world and eternity must impress the translator to make the very best choice. Try to imagine what they are translating and their obvious commitment to it.

Bible translation is taken for granted by many in the English-speaking world, though there might be an occasional argument over which translation is better than another. It is a wonderful luxury that English speakers enjoy—a multitude of translations. But there are many people in the world who do not have any Bibles in their own language. Countless groups work tirelessly to translate Scripture in unreached languages. In the first millennium of the Common Era (abbreviated herein CE and referring to the years from 1 CE forward), the Bible had been translated into fewer than 20 languages (not including dialects). The second millennium has seen a burgeoning of translations into thousands of languages, each with a stirring story of dedication, resolve, and suffering and a huge amount of charitable giving to support these works.

Operating in cooperation with these groups at the grass roots are national Bible societies such as the American Bible Society, the oldest nonprofit in America, established in 1816. There are also international confederations. These nonsectarian (meaning they are not associated with any particular Judeo-Christian organization) groups distribute translations, sponsor new translations, and work to inspire Bible readership.

The point made poignantly in the Translators' Station is that the story of the Bible is not isolated to one particular translation. Unlike Islam, in Christianity there is a celebration of translations and an encouragement to think critically and to discern the differences among them. The Bible is a living book with a living and relevant message that regenerates itself through the means of translation. This room reveals an essential part of the story, showing the ongoing process of translation. Having the entire Bible, or portions of it, translated into every language and dialect on earth is within reach. There is truly something remarkably different about this book called the Bible.

CHAPTER SIXTEEN

A POSTSCRIPT: THE FINAL THEATER

Before the exit of *Passages*, a final theater tells the story of the composition and transmission of the most influential book ever written. The story is told in the words of the Bible—plain and simple. The emphasis is on the transmission of the text. As illustrated throughout *Passages*, the Bible was preserved through immense toil and care, at tremendous expense, even loss of life, by two great monotheistic faiths—Judaism and Christianity. The film depicts the transmission of the text over time and across the world like a runner with a baton-like scroll. One generation and culture passes the message on to another.

The word *tradition* comes from a Latin root which means "to pass along by hand." In this technological age, the Bible can be accessed from the Internet, or on a phone "app" effortlessly in the most remote places on earth. It is a remarkable time. Technological developments are of enormous importance and, like Gutenberg's press, have driven the dissemination of the Bible. But technology can also detach someone from the process of and an appreciation for the transmission and preservation of the Bible. The short film encapsulates the story told in *Passages*. It ends with a runner handing the scroll to the audience because, after all, what one chooses to do with this Book of Books is an individual decision.

Special displays will also be featured throughout the months that *Passages* will be on exhibit. Those displays include a stunning selection of Jewish religious art illustrating communal and private faith, illuminated manuscripts, icons and other items from an Ethiopic Royal Library, and a wide variety of Books of Hours, to name a few. Each is worth a visit so, by all means, come back again, if you can.

Thank you for spending time in *Passages: The 400th Anniversary of the King James Bible* and learning about the composition, transmission, preservation, adornment, and dissemination of the most copied, most printed, most banned, most controversial, and most influential book of all times. We trust your visit has brought you a new appreciation for its place in culture and art.

PICTORIAL INDEX

PICTORIAL INDEX

Photo Credit: Al Levine Photography, Atlanta

Visitor docents, 2
Docent monk, 13
St. Jerome's Cave, 21
St. Jerome's Lion, 22
St. Jerome at work, 23
Peasant docents (2), 34
Salesman docent, 35
Reformation Theater, 55
Theater, 56
Debate docent, 56
Eck docent, 57
Erasmus docent, 57
Luther docent, 57, 64
Boleyn throne room, 73
Boleyn dungeon, 74
Lady docent, 75
Tyndale at stake, 85
Knox's Chapel, 91
John Knox, 92
Usher docent, 93
Beefeater docent, 103
Royal Print Shop, 111-112
Laborer docent, 113
Artist docent, 121
Translator Station, 142
Final Theater, 145